W9-BXE-487

# Catholic Identity After Vatican II

# Catholic Identity After Vatican II

## Three Types of Faith in the One Church

Frans Jozef van Beeck, S.J.

Loyola University Press
Chicago 60657

*Imprimi potest*
John J. Begley, S.J.,
Acting Provincial, New England Province
Boston, August 24, 1983



Printed and bound in the United States of America

Library of Congress Cataloging in Publication Data

Beeck, Frans Jozef van.
Catholic identity after Vatican II

1. Catholic Church—History—1965- . 2. Catholic Church—Doctrines—History—20th century. 3. Identification (Religion)—History—20th century. I. Title.
BX1390.B4 1985 282′.09′048 85-13058
ISBN 0-8294-0498-8

For Pedro Arrupe, S.J.,
General of the Society of Jesus,
1965-1983
Man of Identity and Openness

# Contents


| | | |
|---|---|---|
| | Foreword | ix |
| ONE | The Catholic Faith and Identity Experience after Vatican II | 1 |
| | Introduction | 1 |
| | Vatican II and the Task of "Rearrangement" | 2 |
| | "Rearrangement" and the Tasks of Theology | 7 |
| | Identity Experience in Transition | 11 |
| | Between Identity and Openness: Negotiation of New Boundaries | 19 |
| TWO | The New Openness and the Problem of Identity | 23 |
| | Introduction | 23 |
| | The Pistic Experience: Backgrounds | 24 |
| | The Pistic Experience: Four Characteristics | 30 |
| | The Charismatic Experience | 34 |
| | Serious Questions | 41 |

Pistics and Charismatics: Common Limitations 46

*THREE* Sharing Life: Mystical Identity in Patience and Hospitality

Introduction: Universality, Eschatology, and Christ's Resurrection 51

The Risen Christ as the Mystical Source of Identity and Mission 55

Worship as the Heart of the Mystical Experience 61

Conclusion: Cultivation of Mysticism 67

Openness in Patience and Hospitality 71

*APPENDIX ONE* Three Levels of Faith-Experience 79

*APPENDIX TWO* Two Examples 83

Rahner's Proposal for Brief Statements of the Faith 83

Vatican Reply to ARCIC I 88

Notes 95

# Foreword

The first encouragement I received to write this little book came in late 1982 in the form of a request for some lectures on ecumenism and evangelization from my dear friend Parmananda Divarkar, S.J., then Director of the Jesuit Secretariate for Ecumenism and Evangelization in Rome.

The agenda of the 1983 General Assembly of the World Council of Churches in Vancouver helped to bring home to me the urgency of the subject. But it was principally the twentieth anniversary of the second Vatican Council that helped me determine what to write. I took my cue, therefore, from Vatican II's concern with the nature of the Church and her relationship to the world. This led me to raise once again two issues very much debated at the council, namely, those of identity and openness. This time, however, they had to be discussed in the light of the experience of twenty years of post-conciliar developments in the Catholic Church—developments which Vatican II could only foresee dimly, if at all, yet developments which it helped to promote.

My participation in the thirty-third General Congregation of the Society of Jesus contributed to the further clarification of my thinking. It was in that congregation that the Jesuit order faced the balance-sheet of its post-conciliar change and renewal; and it was also in that congregation that it gratefully accepted the resignation of its post-conciliar General, Father Pedro Arrupe, to whom I am dedicating this little book.

If Vatican II did anything, it created movement where there had been, in the view of many, monumental immobility. These chapters study one ingredient of this movement, namely, the fact that faith comes in more than one shape, which in turn produces varieties of Catholic experience of identity and openness. This new Catholic consciousness of the availability of variety, sometimes called pluriformity, does not content itself with having various forms of faith coexist side by side in the Church. Variety and movement have combined to produce new and unforeseen transitions and developments, and the evaluation of these has hardly begun.

These new developments, I believe, need and deserve and indeed demand empathetic and critical theological attention and evaluation. We can only neglect them at the risk of jeopardizing the development of a new phase in the Catholic Church's tradition of worship, life, and teaching, to which must correspond a new spiritual-pastoral-theological synthesis. It is appropriate, therefore, that the publication of this volume coincides with the special Synod of Bishops called by Pope John Paul II to study twenty years of post-conciliar development.

If this little book is defective, it is not so for lack of much-appreciated encouragement from the Roberts House Jesuit community and the Department of Theology at Boston College. I am also grateful for the friendly criticisms of Mark Santer, Mary Tanner, and my fellow Jesuits Ben de Bock and Robert J. Daly.

Finally, movement, variety, development, and transition are exactly what these chapters incorporate in yet another, more personal way. Although they were written at Boston College, these chapters are my inaugural lectures in the John Cardinal Cody Chair of Theology at Loyola University of Chicago. And yet, no transition occurs without deep continuity, symbolized, in this case, by the Jesuit idea of a university in the service of identity and openness in the Catholic Church.

Frans Jozef van Beeck, S.J.
Boston College, Spring 1985

# ONE

# The Catholic Faith and Identity Experience After Vatican II

## Introduction

These three chapters propose to deal with two issues which were at the heart of the second Vatican Council, and which the recent General Assembly of the World Council of Churches at Vancouver, British Colombia, has once again forcefully called to mind. They are perennial issues, which the Church cannot afford to omit from her agenda for reflection, self-examination, and prayer. The first issue is ecumenism, that is, the Church's concern with the graces and the failures of her unity and diversity. The second issue is evangelization, that is, the Church's concern with the graces and the failures of her universal mission.

At the second Vatican Council, these questions took the shape of two major themes: the Church's identity *ad intra* and her mission *ad extra*—themes which the Council, in a dramatic fashion, adopted as its agenda twenty years ago, contrary to the expectations of many. The two themes are, of course, intimately related, and in the final analysis they are identical: the life that we share in Christ demands that it be shared with the world. The Church must mediate: she has to do justice, in the Spirit, to the One God and Father of Jesus Christ, just as she must do justice to the world she lives in. The former must be the source, both of her identity and of her mission; the latter must be the very stuff she is made of, which she must assume and welcome, and which she must engage in in order to find the way home to God. In dealing with ecumenism and evangelization, therefore, we are dealing with central theological issues.

## Vatican II and the Task of "Rearrangement"

If we propose to deal with Vatican II and some of its central questions, this will be, first of all, an exercise in historical realism. It is not an *obbligato* performance imposed by a sense of loyalty, nor do we expect theological miracles from the treatment; and least of all do we expect to have our thoughts raised far above the fray of history. Councils themselves are not miraculous; they are firmly beholden to the laws and vicissitudes of historical process. Vatican II is as firmly located in history as any other event which the Christian consciousness accepts as significant. But councils (and some councils more than others!) *are* symbolic events; they are celebrated rather than just organized—something the Preparatory Commissions of Vatican II had occasion to find out! And precisely because they are celebrated they develop a curious, concentrated intensity, which brings about an acceleration, or as some might say, a "contraction," of history, which is typical of symbolic events. This is what gives them their strong significance, prospectively as well as retrospectively. One could compare them with the nodal points of a vibrating string: while motionless themselves, they set the condition for the movement on either side of them. Hence, to take Vatican II seriously is tantamount to taking stock of the faith-developments that led up to it, as well as projecting the agenda set for the Catholic faith for the foreseeable future, and a large agenda it is.

To make this claim, we do not also have to claim that Vatican II is in all respects a theological masterpiece. Some of its documents are better than others, and none are perfect—few documents ever are.[1] Vatican II, therefore, does not provide us with any perfect synthesis. We are still underway, *in via*; we have not yet arrived.

But it remains true that Vatican II did involve itself in serious reflection on the Church, that is to say, on the Church's *identity*, her *nature*; and in doing so, the Council found it impossible not to take cognizance of the issue of *openness*, her *mission* to the world. It started by approaching both Church and world in a positive way, true to Pope John XXIII's confident program of *aggiornamento*. In this way, the other Christian churches and ecclesial communities were taken seriously, as was Judaism. The great religions and their inherent values were fairly acknowledged, as was the emerging consciousness of the dignity and the rights of the human person. Accordingly, the Council produced the texts on ecumenism, on Judaism, on the non-Christian religions, on the Church's missionary activity, and on freedom of religion, and last but not least, the Pastoral Constitution on the Church in the Modern World, *Gaudium et Spes,* perhaps the most ambitious undertaking of them all.

We have grown accustomed to these documents over the past two decades, even to the point where familiarity may have bred some contempt. And yet we would do well to remember that Vatican II succeeded in dealing, as a matter of fact, with no less than four centuries' worth of religious and cultural development full of conflict, and that it eventually came to terms, in a prophetic manner, with the fact that the Catholic Church is now, for the first time in history, actually faced with the challenge of becoming a global Church, as Karl Rahner has argued.[2] The past it dealt with was a difficult past, but the Council dealt with it in a constructive way. It acknowledged the

Reformation, thus doing justice to the great, and often painful, theological and ecclesial developments of the sixteenth and seventeenth centuries. It acknowledged the great world religions, which first began to strike the newly-enlightened fancy of the West in the late seventeenth and early eighteenth centuries. It took seriously humanity's deep aspirations to freedom and religiosity, and the human individual's threatened integrity, dignity, and conscience—some of the deepest anthropological concerns of the Enlightenment. It acknowledged, with admiration as well as a healthy critical sense, the astounding developments brought about by four centuries of cultivation and application of scientific and technological reason, in the material world as well as in the human family. And more themes could be added to this list.

This summary of past events should lead to a conclusion, one which will be the subject of the first part of this first chapter. It could be formulated as follows. Vatican II, in taking four centuries of religious and cultural developments seriously in a novel fashion, and in facing up to an unprecedented global challenge, must be understood to have *inaugurated a significant rearrangement of the themes and emphases of the Catholic faith and identity experience*.

If this looks like a truism more than twenty years after the opening ceremony, three comments may be appropriate.

First, Vatican II, as we just said, *inaugurated* a significant rearrangement; *inaugurated*, not *completed*. Vatican II did not give us a finished synthesis, but a *mandate*; the Council of two decades ago presents us with an unfinished agenda today.

Secondly, Vatican II inaugurated a rearrangement of "the themes and emphases of the Catholic faith and identity experience"; not "themes and emphases of Catholic theology." What Vatican II envisaged was a renewal of the *Church*, and only indirectly a renewal of theology. In our day, with its immoderate regard for technical expertise, this reminder that faith and theology, though usually related, are not identical, may not be out of place.[3] It takes more than good theology to renew the Church, no matter how fruitful and even decisive the contribution of the theological *periti* at the Council turned out to be. We will have to come back to this point later on.

Thirdly, Vatican II inaugurated "a significant rearrangement" of the themes and emphases of the Catholic faith-experience. This third theme must be elaborated at greater length.

Let us start with a quotation from John Henry Newman's Tract 73 of 1835, *On the Introduction of Rationalistic principles into Revealed Religion.* Christian Revelation, Newman says, ". . . is not a revealed *system*, but consists of a number of detached and incomplete truths belonging to a vast system unrevealed, of doctrines and injunctions mysteriously connected together." And he concludes that ". . . considered as a mystery," Revelation is "a doctrine lying *hid* in language."

What this means, among other things, is that no faith-expression gives an adequate account, either of the integral act of faith, or of its content, its motives, or its significance. There is always more to be said, which means: there is always a lot that is left unsaid. In fact, *positive* attempts at "unsaying" are part and parcel of the language of faith. And in any case, whether there are things simply left unsaid or things positively unsaid, the language of faith must appeal to the imagination to become true in the full sense and to show its coherence.[4]

In what was just said about the *language* of faith, we may seem to have given excessive attention to doctrine. "Faith-expression," as a matter of fact, takes place not only in Creed, but also in Conduct and in Cult. The experience of faith is a living tradition embodied in "doctrine, life, and worship," as Vatican II explained.[5] In the *language* of faith, much remains unsaid; in parallel fashion, *the Christian commitment to the good life* involves behavioral commitments too deep to be entirely brought to the surface, and while the Church's *worship*, which is her response to God's Presence, does indeed prompt her every word and gesture of prayer, the basic act of worship eludes the grasp of those who pray.[6]

Precisely because of the eloquence of the unspoken, the urgency of the unattained, and the awesomeness of the ungrasped, the history of faith-expression resembles those well-known maps of the world that show the history of continental drift: both the continuity and the discontinuity are obvious. The configuration of the continents is now vastly different from what it once was; some parts that were once joined together have now come apart, and *vice versa*; some parts that were once submerged have now come to the surface, and *vice versa*. And yet, while the patterns of prominence and recessiveness, of connection and separation are greatly altered, it is recognizably the same earth. Some features of the faith which were "hid" in the Christian language of ages past have recently been brought to the surface for the first time; for instance, the statement that the Jews as a people cannot be blamed for the execution of Jesus. Other features, recessive for a long time, have resurfaced; for instance, the conviction that the liturgy and the scriptures must be available in the vernacular, a conviction cherished by many of our separated brethren long before Vatican II.

Let us go back to the main point. Vatican II must be understood to have inaugurated a significant rearrangement of the themes and emphases of the Catholic faith-experience. The entire, very coherent, doctrinal-moral-liturgical arrangement which was inaugurated, let us say, by the Council of Trent, and which enjoyed its last embattled conciliar moment of glory at Vatican I, is now to be reinterpreted. This reinterpretation will have to take place in the light of a council which adopted a different, and in some respects even opposite, arrangement of themes and emphases, a council which in any case enjoyed a totally different, namely global, perspective.

Now the contention of this chapter is, as we indicated, that the work of this rearrangement has only just begun. Some among us will remember the widespread euphoria that developed during and immediately after the council; the New Church seemed to be just around the corner. We were, in retrospect, a bit naive about the dynamics of history; renewals of the kind inaugurated by Vatican II tend to involve a long period of difficult, though often creative, ferment. We should add, for the record, that a similar kind of historical shortsightedness and naiveté is sometimes found in neo-traditionalist quarters, when it is suggested that a simple return to canon law and order can stem the tide of ferment. The historic change of perspective embraced by Vatican II cannot be so quickly captured and operationalized by a few stabilizing institutional procedures and by appeals to loyalty and obedience.

Why insist on this? Two main reasons suggest themselves. The first is positive. The rearrangement under discussion involves the *entire* Catholic community. This means that it must be a process of widespread inner growth, and growth across cultural boundaries to boot. Such processes take time.

The second is partly negative, and it concerns the role of theology in the task of the rearrangement under discussion. This subject is of some importance for the purposes of these chapters; it deserves to be discussed at greater length.

## "Rearrangement" and the Tasks of Theology

We have witnessed for some time now what may fairly be considered an exaggeration of the importance of theology viewed as an authoritative instrument for the promotion of either stability or change in the Church. Now it is understandable that, in the excitement of Vatican II, theology was credited with great power of clarification and even change. Council Fathers on either side of the conservative-liberal divide were largely agreed on this, even though they had contrary appreciations of the fact. Still, it seems more realistic, historically speaking, to cast the theologians prominent at the Council in the role, not so much of *originators* of a new faith-experience, as of *mouthpieces* of religious and cultural experiences that had been repressed far too long by the siege mentality of a Catholic Church long ill at ease both with the world she was living in *and with herself.* This has been borne out by the postconciliar outburst of activity, some of it nervous abreaction, some of it productive ferment.

There *have*, of course, been very important theological developments. But we should remember that Rahner and Lonergan attained their prominence and their influence, not because they were doing theology, but because they were doing theology *well*. They succeeded in coming to terms with religious and cultural experiences too long repressed in the Church as we knew her, and they showed that there was ultimately nothing to fear and much to gain from the basic concerns of the Enlightenment (Rahner) and of the modern, differentiated, empirical approach to the world and humanity (Lonergan). In the same way, Congar, de Lubac, Daniélou, and Urs von Balthasar, while doing theology, proved to an anxious ecclesiastical establishment that the landscape of the Catholic faith had *de facto* looked very different in the authoritative past without being any the less Catholic for it, and that a strong sense of Catholic identity was entirely compatible with a positive, appreciative openness to the processes and products of culture.

Still, good theology is *not directly*, but only indirectly, associated with the bringing about of either ecclesiastical stability or change. The awkward, though frequent, question, “Are you a conservative theologian or a liberal one?” is ominous, precisely because of the underlying association of theology with the politics of ecclesiastical authority or power. The real question is, “How good a theologian are you?” That question has everything to do with conscientiousness in dealing both with the Church's Tradition, including Scripture, and with the world the Church exists in. It has nothing to do with unhistorically canonizing yesterday's shape of the Church (or, for that matter, any day's), or with advocating the overthrow of today's shape.

The theologian's first loyalty, then, is to the Church's historic Tradition as a whole. The postconciliar rearrangement of themes and emphases of the Catholic faith and identity experience will precisely consist in the furthering of this continuing, historic Tradition. To use the words of the second Vatican Council, it will have to occur in the "teaching, life, and worship" of the living, historic community, in "all that [the Church] herself is, all that she believes."[7] Good theology can be of considerable help in the process of handing on and furthering this living, historic Tradition, in testing and guiding the entire Catholic community's inner growth.

It can do so in three ways.

The Church is appointed to mediate between God and the world. This takes the form of Tradition, the living process by which the themes and emphases of the faith-experience arrange and rearrange themselves. The heartbeat of this process moves on the rhythm, sometimes fast, sometimes slow, of systole and diastole. The Church can only give life *to* the world if she also expands to take in the life *of* the world. The Church can speak to the culture with authority only if she has a developed power of assimilation by which cultural elements once foreign to her are integrated.[8]

The theologian's task in this process is discretionary. Sometimes—and this is *the first way*—he or she will have to represent the concerns of the world, the surrounding culture, the concerns yet to be integrated into the Christian faith-experience. One is reminded of the young Aquinas, determined to integrate the power of formal thinking into the experience of faith. At other times—*the second way*—he or she will have to represent the basic experience out of which the Church lives, and he or she will have to recall the Church to herself. We may recall Karl Barth's reminder that the theologian's first task is to remind the Church of her "original and normative nature," her true identity. In our own day, Hans Urs von Balthasar, no stranger to Barth himself, has called our attention to the same theme. At *all* times—and this is *the third way*—the theologian must study and test the present arrangement of the faith-experience's themes and emphases, as it is situated between Church and world, worship and worldliness, witness and willingness to listen and learn.

The remainder of this chapter and all of the next one will be mainly devoted to the third of these three ways. We are to study, briefly, the situation in which the Catholic Church finds herself as she faces the task of developing a new arrangement of themes and emphases in the Catholic attitude of openness to other Christian Churches and to the world at large. In the third chapter, our principal approach will be mainly based on the second of the three ways indicated. We will concentrate on the basic Christian faith and identity experience, and then go on to show what attitudes in the area of ecumenism and evangelization are warranted, and indeed mandated, by that experience.

For the moment, though, let us sum up.

Positively, we have seen that Vatican II has mandated and inaugurated a rearrangement of the themes and emphases of the Catholic faith-experience. That such a rearrangement is *a priori* not only possible, but even likely, is based on the insight that *all* expressions of faith-experience, *in and of themselves*, are a matter of configurative balance between what is said and what is unsaid. No expression of faith-experience, in other words, is ever exhaustive or final. In addition, there is the fact that the shaping of faith-experience is the result of an *historic, ongoing* exchange between Church and world, which accounts for the fact that faith-expression occurs in a succession of arrangements—the Church's living Tradition of teaching, life, and worship.[9]

Negatively, we have seen that theology as a discipline is not going to be the principal instrument of this rearrangement, let alone its principal subject. The historic, organic always-to-be-reformed Church community is. But at the same time, the theological achievements around the time of Vatican II and since remain important because they have constructively dealt with four centuries of cultural and religious experience kept largely outside the Catholic Church, and there is no reason to doubt the uses of good theology in the future.

Finally, these chapters promise to concentrate on two theological tasks, namely, the task of testing present arrangements, and the task of representing the Church's basic identity as it reflects on ecumenism and evangelization.

## Identity Experience in Transition

Vatican II inaugurated, but did not complete, a fresh arrangement of the themes and emphases of the Catholic faith-experience. This implies, among other things, that the new elements in its decrees are not likely to be in perfect harmony with the elements derived from the tradition. This, of course, does not apply to all the documents in the same way. Thus, for instance, chapters 1 and 2 of *Lumen Gentium* and most of the Decree on the Church's Missionary Activity, *Ad Gentes*, are among the best-integrated and most mature of all the Council's documents. The worshipful, confident, and sober-minded[10] expression of the Church's identity gives rise, almost effortlessly, to a positive account of the Catholic Church's perspective on, and her relationships with, other Christian Churches and Communities, the Jews, Islam, the great religions, and the various types of unbelievers. At other points, however, the tone and the structure of the documents are hesitant; they betray compromise rather than integration. The history of the Catholic Church's relationships with all the groups mentioned has been full of conflict. Hence we can expect to find that the latter, more compromise-oriented passages reflect the *actual* situation in the Church rather than the former. The old conflicts are past, but we are still at odds with ourselves and with our newly-discovered friends. The "separated brethren" and the non-Christian world still appear to the Catholic perception as strangers rather than relatives.

Once again, this is not hard to understand in the light of history. The Catholic Church's concern with non-Catholics and non-Christians did not, as a matter of historical fact, arise from an *inner* urge to meet and encounter them appreciatively. Rather, their importance was brought home largely from the outside–it was no longer possible to oppose them, let alone ignore them. Note the expression: "*no longer* possible." Vatican II's fresh approach to ecumenism and its new conception of evangelization was long overdue in the eyes of many of the Council Fathers. This presumably echoed the feelings of the vast majority of Catholics. Many people experienced a sense of lag; and this was, perhaps, the best indication that ecumenism and evangelization indeed dawned upon the Church from outside rather than growing out of an inner, urgent conviction. The other churches and the world at large *demanded* attention, and eventually it was given to them. But it was not volunteered, at least not corporately. John Courtney Murray was right in pointing out that the Council's Declaration on Religious Freedom was "hardly . . . a milestone in human history–moral, political or intellectual. . . . In all honesty it must be admitted that the Church is late in acknowledging the validity of the principle." And he goes on to point out that "the real sticking-point," which "continually lay below the surface of the conciliar debates" and which "still remains to be explained by theologians," is "the issue of the development of doctrine."[11] We need only compare the *Syllabus errorum* of 1864 with the documents of Vatican II to notice the striking difference and to realize that a lot of explaining still remains to be done if we are to make sense of the fact that *both* are part of

Catholic history. Still, we may surmise that while making theological, intellectual sense of the changes in the area of *doctrine* is certainly difficult, as Murray suggests, the task of clarifying the common, shared faith-*experience* is likely to be even harder.

Part of the widespread fascination with the late Cardinal Ottaviani during and after the Council was probably due to the fact that, while representing everything that was foreign to the developing faith-experience of numerous realistic Catholics, he also represented the faith-experience that had given them identity and stability. Thus he gained symbolic significance; he became the symbol of an inner conflict. Along with his motto, *Semper Idem*, he represented everything that the Church, the diocese, the parish, the Catholic school, the trade union, and the individual Catholic had for a long time been relying on (though on account of it many had also left the Catholic Church). He was also living proof of the conviction that the Catholic Church could not possibly go on in this vein. Characteristically, and we might add symbolically also, the Council's "liberals" were *many* in number. They represented the felt need to deal with a great variety of concerns which Catholics had to catch up on–the separated brethren and the non-Christian world being among the most obvious. The widely perceived polarization between Ottaviani and the "good guys," between "conservatives" and "liberals," was, therefore, at least partly a projective product of the *uneasy conscience* of average Catholics (a category that included many priests and religious and bishops!). They wanted to remain Catholics and yet get out of the ghetto, to be Catholics and yet stop feeling guilty or clumsy about their associations with Protestants, Jews, and unbelievers. And they wanted to distance themselves from a style of missionary activity which now seemed, in retrospect, to have been excessively associated with a colonialism and an imperialism that were firmly dated by the emergence of independent nations everywhere.

Willem van de Pol, therefore, was on target when in 1966 he opened his thought-provoking book *The End of Conventional Christianity*[12] with a pointer on *prejudice*. The structure of the traditional Catholic faith-experience bore a formal resemblance to the structure of prejudice, so ably analysed by Gordon Allport.[13] And one thing that happened at Vatican II was the open admission of the cognitive and practical dissonance experienced by Catholics everywhere between their monolithic sense of Catholic identity on the one hand and their openness to the non-Catholic world on the other. This discovery brought into the open those features of the Catholic experience that were associated with prejudice.

It is important to note the expression: "features . . . *associated with* prejudice." It would obviously be a mistake to call the traditional Catholic experience simply a complex of prejudices. But there was a real problem, and it was one of *lack of differentiation*. Let us take an example. Such a shrewd and practical man as the late Cardinal Heenan tended to lump a number of different features of the Catholic experience together under the heading of "distinguishing marks," like "Mass on Sunday, fish on Friday." This undifferentiated, paternalistic way of speaking clearly supported the prejudicial structure of the Catholic experience, because of its lack of emphasis on, and education in, a hierarchy of truths and values. So when the reaction against paternalism came, it was, understandably, equally undifferentiated and quite adolescent. If "fish on Friday" could go, how about "Mass on Sunday"? Or, to take an extreme, yet often heard example: If Adam and Eve were not historical, how about Jesus? Average Catholics, with an average or even better-than-average education, lacked two things. First, they did not have the tools to differentiate reliably between what was central and what was peripheral, between faith and prejudice. And secondly, they were unaware of the lessons of history, as they were unaware of the work of great minds like Henri Bremond, Charles Moeller, or Hans Urs von Balthasar–representatives of the long-standing, very Catholic tradition of unprejudiced, yet critical *openness* to the culture.

It makes sense in this context to point to a related example. The concept of "anonymous Christianity" functions, in Karl Rahner's theology, as one of the guarantees of the conviction that far from being a naive or sectarian prejudice, the Catholic and Christian faith is the gracious fulfillment of the deepest aspirations of the human person. In this way, the concept authorizes the Church's openness to the world *as well as the relevance of her message to the world*. Now the curious thing is that the concept of "anonymous Christianity" has been taken by some to mean that Rahner is denying the importance of confessional, explicit faith, as if Rahner was saying, "You need not be a Christian, since, really, every good person is basically a Christian anyway." This serious misinterpretation is explicable only if it is assumed that "being a Christian" is still widely experienced as a prejudice that estranges a person from non-Christians. Eager to establish connections with the world, some Catholics have read into Rahner's theology a warrant for their *own* secret wish to free themselves from the kind of Christian identity that embarrasses them.[14]

The new openness to the world that was thrust upon the Catholic Church, was by and large something we were not ready for. So when we opened ourselves to the world, the world taught us a lesson; we had to learn not so much to *protect* our convictions as to *deepen* them–especially those faith-convictions that are central, that is to say, *capable* of being deepened in and of themselves. This is an urgency both for the so-called ordinary faithful and for the theologians. Let us take another example.

The confession of the uniqueness of Jesus Christ has been a feature of the Christian faith from the beginning. To quote one passage among many in the New Testament: "There is salvation in no one else, for God has given people no other name to invoke through which they are to be saved."[15] But ever since the eighteenth century, with its "prejudice against prejudice," succeeded in pushing Christian orthodoxy into the sectarian corner, Christian thinkers in many quarters have been under enormous pressure to give up the affirmation of Christ's uniqueness. In this they were often motivated by a thoroughly traditional Christian eagerness to communicate the faith to "the cultured despisers of religion." The doctrine of Christ's uniqueness has even been characterized as an unacceptable, because neuroticizing, warrant for aggression, because it allegedly commits the orthodox Christian to the defense of him who did not defend himself (Thomas Szasz, echoing Celsus and even Lucretius); as nothing but the theological expression of the unacceptable thesis of Western superiority—the foundation of colonialism and imperialism; as nothing but the theological rationalization of male dominance; as nothing but the Christian equivalent of Buddhism's reverence or the Buddha, and so on.[16]

There are conscientious theologians [17] who have felt justified in trading faith in the uniqueness of Jesus Christ for openness to other religions. Theirs may have been an extreme reaction, but this was *de facto* the choice they saw themselves faced with. This is a vivid illustration of the dilemma that many orthodox, conscientious Christians have found themselves in. Once the non-Christian world, with all its attractiveness, has impinged upon their social and individual lives, they find themselves facing the alternative either to uphold without qualification the Church and the faith, and to look upon what is outside as questionable, or even as only apparently good (Augustine's *splendida vitia*!), *or* to acknowledge the claims of the outside world and to consent to sacrificing some elements of their former assurance, such as the confession of the uniqueness of Jesus Christ.

A similar tendency has occurred in the area of ecumenism. The "anti-Roman affect," identified—and, I might add, too easily censured—by Hans Urs von Balthasar,[18] is a symptom of a real tension. Seeking good, healthy relations with non-Catholic Christians is bound to put pressure on a Catholic's devotion to, and understanding of, the papacy and the way it is exercised. And analogous things could also be said in regard to the Eucharist and the ordained ministry, to mention only two other subjects on which Protestants and Catholics, for all their *rapprochement*, are still divided.

Cardinal Ottaviani symbolized the traditional establishment and the sense of identity it provided. For him, the Church could never allow herself to be displaced by claims foreign to her, except when forced to do so; error has no rights. Ecumenism, openness to world religions, and the affirmation of religious freedom could never be more than a matter of unavoidable compromise. Hence they were a matter of *practical* necessity, never of principle. Openness (in the sense of receptiveness) was a *concession*, not a choice. While the integrity of *individual* non-Catholics was worthy of respect, non-Catholic *establishments*, such as churches, religions, and theologically neutral political and social establishments, while tolerable in practice, could never be positively valued. The Church could never mislead her own members, or anybody for that matter, where the truth was concerned.

Ottaviani, the super-Catholic, did not stand alone. In fact, he had a curious, though very important, counterpart across the ecclesiastical border, namely, Karl Barth. The latter did not leave anybody in doubt about the firmness of his rejection of Roman Catholicism, especially the type of Catholicism represented by Ottaviani, which he viewed as an unwarrantable attempt to tie the sovereign gracious freedom of God down to a politico-ecclesiastical, clerical establishment that canonizes itself and forces people to trade in the obedience of faith for ecclesiastical obedience. Still, paradoxically, the two had a basic concern in common, even though Barth's theological vision was much deeper and much more original than Ottaviani's, who was personally something of a Last Hurrah.[19] Both men passionately agreed that the Church must *protest*, and that she will only make herself acceptable to the outside world at her own peril, that is, at the risk of losing her integrity and identity.[20] Ecumenism must never compromise that integrity; nor must the Church, in her efforts at evangelization, ever create the impression that the general category of "religion" provides a comfortable meeting-ground between Christian faith and world religions.[21] While upholding the possibility of salvation for *individual* non-Christians—*extra ecclesiam nulla salus* does not commit the Church to the belief that all those outside of it are damned—non-Christian *establishments* can only be credited with saving power at the expense of the Church's own sense of mission—and that price is too high.

Relatively few Catholics (to leave other Christians aside for the moment) put the issue in terms as radical as Ottaviani and Barth were prepared, at least in theory, to put it. But all Catholics experienced the problem of Christian identity in similar terms. Even in countries where the closed-Church system was not supported by concordats or other political devices, and where the Church was living in a pluralistic society, the Catholic Church had generated a rather firm framework of "distinguishing marks," some more substantial than others, and some more productive than others, which served to tie the Catholic faith-experience to the experience of firm *boundaries*.

Vatican II's recognition of the separated brethren and the non-Christians changed the nature of the boundaries, and hence, the nature of the Catholic faith-experience: Catholic identity no longer excluded a positive approach to ecumenism and evangelization. But this change in focus which was brought about by Vatican II called for the elaboration of a new, very precarious balance between Catholic identity and openness. And this balance, it would appear to many, requires a process of the most careful *negotiation*.

## Between Identity and Openness: Negotiation of New Boundaries

If Vatican II was a conversion experience for the Catholic Church, it was not a rash one. The Council documents are proof of the painstaking care with which the new orientations were joined to the older traditions. Even more painfully deliberate were the ways in which the post-conciliar commissions began to put the conciliar decrees into effect (or, as some would have it, began to betray them). The boundaries of the past had to be abandoned in the interest of the new openness, and the first move was a careful attempt to negotiate new boundaries.

What happened in accelerated time during and immediately after Vatican II among bishops and *periti* (and, we may suppose, journalists and their reading public) must now be lived out by the *entire* community in *real* time: "the jading and jar of the cart, Time's tasking."[22] This process is likely to be carried along on the tide of risktaking and withdrawal, expansion and contraction, exhilaration and disappointment, consolation and desolation, integration and disintegration. This is how the rearrangement of the themes and emphases of the Catholic faith-experience is being worked out, as we have been able to observe, in ecumenism as well as in evangelization. Ecumenism has given us quite a few consensus statements full of promise; but disappointingly, they do not secure the broad acceptance they deserve. In the area of evangelization we have seen indigenization and inculturation equally full of promise in many places; but they, too, are often followed by sharp retrenchments and rebukes.

All of this shows two things.

First, for the time being *we must reckon with the likelihood of a continued process of negotiation to achieve a new balance between identity and openness*. This process is not likely to be an elegant, nicely balanced exercise all the time or everywhere. In fact, there are places where the boundaries of the past used to be unusually sharp, and where the practicing rate among Catholics used to be very high, and where, in addition, the Vatican Council coincided with major shifts in the socio-economic-political area; places like French Canada and the Netherlands come to mind. In those places "negotiation" tends to look more like a violent lurching between extremes than a dialectic seeking a new integration between identity and openness.

Can some kind of real balance between identity and openness be achieved? The theme of the Vancouver Assembly of the World Council of Churches, which is none other than the central theme of the Pauline and Johannine writings, implies that it can, in the confident statement: "Jesus Christ—Life of the World." The first part declares the Christian identity, the latter the Christian openness. What we have here is not a mere evangelistic slogan but the basic Christian conviction that Jesus Christ is the key to all that exists: "everything was made through him, and nothing was made without him,"[23] and "in him all things were created, in heaven and on earth, visible and invisible, whether thrones or dominations or principalities or authorities—all things were created through him and for him. He is before all things and in him all things hold together."[24] But if it is confessed that the Incarnate Lord is the Life of the world, then the Church whose head and beginning he is must count on having to follow the developmental laws of life in this world. And one of these laws is the law which Teilhard de Chardin has called complexification: developing life is capable, by its ever increasing complexity, of opening up to and embracing and assimilating ever more foreign matter, while at the same time developing higher forms of inner, organic unity.[25] The dialectic of identity and openness is part of the Church's vocation to be the continuing and living incarnation of Him through whom and with whom and in whom the whole universe came, comes, and will come alive to the Father.

But it also shows something else, and this is the second point: *the question of Catholic identity must be asked anew*. We have already seen that the compromise-oriented passages in Vatican II find themselves between the same book covers as the confident, integrated ones. In the same way, the precarious faith-experience I have just described must be placed in the light of the original, abiding, and all-encompassing Catholic and Christian faith-experience. This is so because the faith-experience associated with boundary-experience, and hence the practice of ecumenism and evangelization as functions of negotiation, must not go unquestioned or unchallenged. The Catholic conscience is uneasy, caught as it is for now *between* identity and openness; but it must seek for the kind of identity that *includes openness as an integral part of itself*, even though there is no short-cut to get there.

While the present unease lasts, there will very likely be impatient efforts to seek relief from the tension of the moment by opting for old-fashioned identity or for total openness. There will very probably also be urgent calls for order and *communio*. Such appeals are very understandable, although they fail to deal with the real issue, which is the attainment of a lived sense of deep identity at the level of faith-experience, which in the last analysis is the only secure basis for *communio* and discipline.

So, while the unease lasts, we should turn to the deeper questions. Desolation is, at heart, one of God's ways to call us to deeper faith. We will not get lost in the search. We can even take comfort from Mother Earth. The rearrangement of the continents on the globe was not a matter of superficial change. Continents drift, but they drift deeply; they do not float.

*TWO*

# The New Openness and the Problem of Identity

## Introduction

Our first chapter ended with a pointer to the task of *deepening* the sense of Catholic identity. This is necessary, we argued, for two interconnected reasons. First, the *new openness* thrust upon the Catholic Church demands that it be matched by a corresponding depth of identity-experience. Developing the new, post-Conciliar arrangement of the themes and emphases of the Catholic faith-experience must be grounded in inner conviction. And secondly, it was argued that we must explore the possibilities of *a sense of identity that is less dependent on boundaries*, which implies that we must explore an approach to openness that is less dependent on negotiation across boundaries. In fact, it was suggested that what we ultimately need is an experience of identity that *includes openness as an integral part of identity itself.*

This chapter will further explore this issue of identity and openness. This will be done in three steps. Firstly, we will further characterize the identity experience associated with boundaries and the openness associated with negotiation. Secondly, we will ask the question as to how the Catholic faith-experience has been affected by the new, post-conciliar openness, and how this development has affected the Catholic attitude in ecumenism and evangelization. Thirdly and finally, we will compare this new experience with the traditional one, and try to evaluate it.

Then, in the third chapter, both the traditional and the new will be examined in light of the original Christian faith and identity experience as the New Testament and the great Tradition have handed it down to us. In this fashion we may discover desirable ways to develop the Catholic faith and identity experience—ways which can also be expected to lead to new forms of ecumenism and evangelization in the future.

## The Pistic Experience: Backgrounds

We will begin with a terminological proposal. Let us retrieve a term from the Greek Fathers and call the traditional Catholic faith-experience which we discussed in the first chapter, 'pistic,' from the Greek word *pistikos,* meaning "faithful," or "believer." Later on, two related terms, also from the patristic tradition, will be introduced to characterize alternative types of faith-experience, namely, 'charismatic' (Gk. *charismatikos*) and 'mystic' (Gk. *mystikos*). Eventually we will argue, at least by implication, that the Christian faith-experience must occur at all three levels in order to be integral.[1]

During the Council it was often said that we were experiencing the end of the Constantinian Era. There were frequent references, also, to the end of the Medieval-Baroque settlement. The meaning of these expressions was clear: *the shape of the Church as Vatican II found it owed a great deal to the Church's history of association with the political facts of the West.* The Theodosian recognition of the church as the State Religion in the fourth century, following the conversion of the emperor Constantine, led to a progressive association of Christian faith with citizenship. This association was strengthened even more by the mass conversion of the Germanic tribes, so much so that some tribes maintained their ethnic identity by theological means. Thus, for instance, under Theodoric and his successors, Arianism functioned as the main expedient to ensure the identity of the Ostrogoths vis-a-vis the old Roman establishment over which they held military sway. This was followed a few centuries later by the association of the Church with the feudal establishment—an association which was durable enough to survive the serious conflicts between the spiritual authorities and the secular arm, from the Emperor and the Pope on down. This same association of Church and political structures would eventually draw the theological debates of the sixteenth and seventeenth centuries firmly into the realm of politics, under the slogan *cuius regio illius et religio*—"the religious affiliation of a country is determined by the religion of its ruler." Even the early Jesuits lived in this world in which church and politics went hand in hand. For all their openness and mobility, they helped to nail down the politico-religious status quo by deliberately locating their colleges along a line—the famous *limes*—which marked, like a theological curtain, the boundary between Catholic and Reformed Europe. St. Robert Bellarmine's concept of the Church as a society which was as visible and structured and perfect *(societas perfecta!)* as the Kingdom of France or the Republic of Venice clinched the association.

No wonder that evangelization, too, came to be understood in political terms, as the spiritual element of a conquest. We are now in a position to regret that the protests of the great Dominican, Bartolomé de las Casas, against the missionary policies of the Spanish Conquista went unheeded. But we have to admit that he and Jesuits like Matteo Ricci and Roberto de Nobili were the exceptions, not the rule. To take another example, the Chinese rites, in retrospect, could hardly have been expected to survive in the context of a missionary strategy that owed so much to the expansionist trade policies of the European monarchies. The North American Jesuit missionaries and martyrs of the mid-seventeenth century may have been scandalized by the greed and immorality of their fellow-Frenchmen, but they could do nothing about the fact that their work of evangelization among the Indians was firmly set in the context of France's massive effort to found a *Nouvelle France*. For them, there was no escape from the traders and the adventurers. In fact, Père Marquette and others positively joined them.

Even in our own day, it is wise to recall a few facts from nineteenth and twentieth century church history. The very political papacy of *Pio Nono* (1846-1878) was instrumental in ensuring the liberty of many Catholic churches in traditionally Catholic countries from the meddling of Febronians and Caesaropapists. To take an example from the Protestant world, while Karl Barth's prophetic protest called the Church away from its association with cultural and political establishments and back to the confession, it very much showed its political potential after 1933, when the protest against the Nazi state and its German Christianity had to be mounted. And in our own day, while we must deplore what the association of the Church with politics has done in Northern Ireland, there is the Polish situation to show us its positive side. And how many of us have not been watching the developments in post-Franco Spain over the past ten years or so with bated breath?

This traditional association of faith with political structures has a counterpart at the level of doctrine, life, and worship. The church's teaching, typically spread by means of catechisms, used to be conceived in terms of *definitions*. Catholic life, with its many distinguishing marks, was strongly regulated by *precepts and commandments*, something that favored the practice of the passive virtues. And the Church's worship was strongly characterized by *rules and obligations and rubrics*.

It is clear that the faith-experience which I have described has strong institutional features. A lot of recent criticism has, unfortunately, focused on exactly these features in and of themselves. But surely there is no such thing as a shapeless, formless life. To believe also means to believe articulately; to behave also means to behave in a responsible and disciplined fashion; to worship also means to act ritually. In fact, the institutional shape of the Church brings home what is of the utmost importance if the Christian faith is to be appreciated for what it is: the Church, the community of the faithful, is an entity that preexists the individual believer, and thus the Church, as a symbolic given, can convey that faith is a gift. Pistic believers, whose attention is not ordinarily diverted by a lot of Ego-needs, tend to have an instinctive appreciation of this fact. Many of them have a spontaneous ability to interpret symbolically (that is to say, realistically!) many structures in the Church which more emancipated, more individualized, and in that sense more motivated, believers experience as prefabricated, restrictive, and alienating. So the problem is not so much with the institution as such as the way in which it is thought of and the way it functions.

This is not to say that there is no serious problem. Two historical points can be offered to clarify this.

The first is an early medieval development. The mass conversions of the Germanic tribes accounted for the *feudal shape of the Latin Church*. This involved the emergence of typically feudal distinctions in the Church, between the leaders and the led, the clergy and the laity, the *dispensatores* of the mysteries and the receivers of them. All of this was given added authority at the time of the so-called Gregorian Reform, in the second half of the eleventh century, when the sharp clergy-laity distinction was reinforced by the distinction between the use of Latin and the vernacular, and increasingly also by the veritable chasm that separated clergy and laity in regard to eucharistic practice. Gone was the ancient, organic *ecclesia-ministeria* structure.[2] The "ordinary faithful" had become, *by definition,* dependent; *the pistic faith and identity experience had become normative.* While historically understandable, this development is *theologically* unnecessary and hence, not authoritative. It was the result of historic events rather than faith-decisions.

The second point concerns certain cultural developments in the mid-sixteenth century which profoundly affected the shape of the institution. These cultural developments in many ways determined the shape of the ecumenical problem as we know it today and the shape of the evangelization problem as it has come down to us. These cultural developments all show an inclination toward a *hardening of boundaries and definitions* unprecedented in the history of the West. In the schools, always places where the ancient practice of dialogue had been observed, much emphasis came to be placed on analysis of concepts and on definitions to develop matter for exposition; Petrus Ramus is the supreme authority here.[3] In the pictorial arts, the laws of optical perspective, which had been characteristically called *costruzione legittima* by Alberti a century before, came to be generally received. Dürer's *Unterweisung der Messung* of 1538, with its emphasis on precise geometrical construction, stands to remind us of that fact. In anatomy, we have the spectacular development of Andreas Vesalius' first "modern" anatomical atlases, the *Tabulae Sex* of 1538 and *De Humani Corporis Fabrica* of 1543, both of them notable for their visual precision and objectivity.[4] Some Thomist commentators in the mid-sixteenth century seem to have started a new tradition in jurisprudence, which not only Suarez and Grotius, but even Spinoza seem to have inherited. They spoke, not so much about natural *law* which lays down the rightness of *things*, as about natural *rights,* which carefully describe and define the rights of certain *persons*, implying that persons are defined and circumscribed by a protective legal barrier.[5] Finally there is Cajetan, who, as de Lubac has shown, replaced Thomas Aquinas' very open understanding of human nature by one taken entirely from Aristotle's nature-philosophy. In thus locking human persons up inside their own "nature," he not only took the first step in the direction of an essentialist understanding of Thomism, but also of a complete juxtaposition of nature and grace, a characteristic shared by much of the Reformation and the Counter-Reformation alike.[6]

All this emphasis on objectivity and definition and analysis, and the corresponding de-emphasizing of dialogue, openness, and synthesis, led to a reduction of truth to truths, of faith to tenets, of Christendom to sovereign monarchies and republics, whose rulers appealed to "divine rights"; and miserably, it also led to the reduction of Church to churches. The post-Tridentine Church, with its simple, straightforward, and almost exclusively *territorial* system of diocesan and parochial jurisdictions, replaced the confusing, but vital pluriformity of the medieval Church, with its many overlapping jurisdictions. In every sphere of life a consistent method of simplification, precision, and absolutizing, practiced evermore *more geometrico*, led to a glorification of boundaries, definitions, and systems that made the institution more and more the prisoner of itself.[7]

These two traditions, that of the normativity of the pistic experience and that of the predominance of what Walter Ong has called the visual, objectifying approach to knowledge and experience—these two traditions have combined to determine the shape of the traditional arrangement of the themes and emphases of the Catholic faith-experience. The first section of this chapter cannot be brought to a conclusion without an enumeration of four characteristics of this traditional arrangement, which we have agreed to call the 'pistic' experience.

## The Pistic Experience: Four Characteristics

The first characteristic to be mentioned must be the phenomenon of *inappropriate lay dependency*. Now what is significant in this is not the phenomenon of dependency in and of itself, for two reasons. First, in every organization there are persons who, at least temporarily, derive more *from* membership than they contribute *to* it. Secondly, as we pointed out already, there is a sense in which *every* member of the Church, including the Pope, must always be dependent on the Church; we keep receiving the faith of the community before we ever contribute to it. But *inappropriate* dependency is something else.

There is another factor to be taken into account. Certain forms of dependency may be deemed appropriate when viewed in the context of historical developments. It is understandable that the uneducated tribesmen around Clovis, who were baptized in one massive wave of "conversion," came to hail Christ, a generation later, and in typically feudal fashion, as "King of the Franks." Only bigotry will misunderstand the blessings of the firm, if very paternalistic, clerical leadership offered to generations of American immigrants of various ethnic backgrounds. It is even possible to understand the educated Catholic intellectuals of the *Actio Catholica* and related movements in the twenties and thirties, and their fierce, if somewhat uncritical, loyalty to the hierarchy and to what they believed was the Tradition.

But dependence of this kind is fast becoming inappropriate, because it is no longer compatible with modern sensibilities. In the objective order, theological as well as political developments are putting an end to the Church's close association with a pre-democratic political order. And more generally, after two world wars devoted to the territorial imperative, we are learning that boundaries are of limited use in the global village. The frontiers in that village between belief and unbelief, right and wrong, leaders and led, insiders and outsiders, judgment and prejudice, national pride and international awareness are all subject to continuous fluctuation. The senselessness of the cold war is more obvious than ever, and this has many people wary of every form of polemics. Ideologies, especially those that are enforced by means of bureaucratic controls, are rightly being discredited. Even in the practice of science, the doctrinaire claims of many scientists of only a few decades ago have given way to the cultivation of openness and modesty and dialogue.

In the same way, we have learned to accept the fact that the Church now exists *in diaspora*, as the expression goes. This means, among many other things, that the Church, like so many voluntary organizations, must now maintain her membership primarily by attraction, not by conformity.[8] This situation makes it liturgically, pastorally, and theologically unacceptable to continue the cultivation of highly detailed ecclesiastical systems that lend theological status to past divisions and past polemics.

These objective developments are matched by corresponding developments in the subjective order. We were used to hearing the praises sung of the "ordinary good Catholic," whose faith tended to find its main focus in the assurance, extended by a strongly institutionalized Church, of the believer's *own salvation*. But this is no longer in tune with the fact that personal independence is everywhere prized, and that passivity is not regarded as a virtue. In fact, if the Church's leadership were to try to *limit* the Christians' faith-experience to the pistic, dependent mode, this would have to be labeled as an undue restriction of the New Testament's clear call for an active, responsible life of Christian virtue on the part of all—a demand very appropriately recalled by *Lumen Gentium* and *Ad Gentes*, which emphasized the universal call to holiness and the missionary vocation of all members of the Church.[9]

Breaking the pistic prejudice can be expected to be a long, arduous task; but fidelity to the Gospel makes it as necessary as the ingrained habits of the past make it difficult. And incidentally, it may be good to recall right at this point that the European Church's feudal past was never part of the experience of large parts of the Catholic Church, not only in the United States and Canada, but especially in Africa, in Indonesia, and elsewhere. Recent converts and their families tend to be motivated, not passive; they tend to think, not only of their own salvation, but also of the salvation of others.

The second point involves another (and again, an unnecessary) characteristic of the pistic experience as it has come down to us in the West. Continuing a tradition of inappropriate dependency keeps alive the old suspicion that Catholicism is *inherently totalitarian and clerical.* While it is certainly right to insist that the Church is not a democracy, we would do well to bear in mind that she is no monarchy either. Some of her monarchical features, in fact, have roots that are historically outdated and theologically very dubious. Congar's contributions to our understanding of the theology of the laity still largely await execution, and a long road it promises to be.

There is a third characteristic of the pistic experience. It is clear that the pistic faith-experience pretty much excluded the traditional believer from the active practice of either ecumenism or evangelization. That role, such as it was, fell to the clergy. But the clergy's main role was defined, not in relation to the other Christian churches or the world, but to the Catholics entrusted to them. It was on the clergy that the pistic believer depended; they were the main guarantors of the Catholic faith and identity experience. Their task involved the teaching of established doctrine and the enforcing of discipline—both of them understood, as explained, in fairly political and objective ways. In the present, post-conciliar situation of flux, one often hears it said that in the traditional situation both doctrine and discipline were in good hands. That may have been so, but it must also be admitted that this tradition had its own shortcomings. There was a selective emphasis on the more objective, that is to say, the more reassuring, themes of the Christian faith: the Incarnation, the objective Atonement, the efficacy of the sacraments, the eucharistic Real Presence, the certainty of the Apostolic Succession and the reliability of its teaching, the objectivity of moral norms, and so forth. All of this very much suited the typical, dependent stance of the pistic believer. But the doctrinal, disciplinary, and liturgical *forms* in which these themes and emphases were presented were so highly defined, and they functioned as such a keen instrument to tell the true from the false brethren that there was little room for real dialogue with other Christians or the outside world, or, for that matter, among the faithful themselves. The traditional pistic faith-experience, in other words, was kept *structurally impatient and inhospitable*.

This leads to a fourth and final characteristic. The pistic experience glorified *the past*. The basic, almost instinctive, ground for this glorification was (and is) that the past is taken to symbolize the eternal order of things. The tradition is taken to guarantee the truth. The problem was (and is) that tradition was understood without much of a real sense of history. Pious revisionism of the pastoral kind reigned supreme: the past history of the Church was largely told with a view to justifying the *present* arrangement of the Catholic faith and identity experience. Past doctrinal developments were hardly recognized, and if they were, their historic significance tended to be minimized. Very seldom was it recognized that some past developments deserve little authority and that their maintenance continues to make new, legitimate developments impossible.[10]

In the wake of Vatian II many of the Catholic Church's former appeals to tradition have been shown to be untenable. They were the result of a defensive, anxious stance of impatience and inhospitality, and of far too *forensic* and judgmental an attitude vis-a-vis the outside world. It was, therefore, a momentous move on Pope John's part to call on Vatican II to trade in judgment for mercy, understanding, and dialogue.[11] Such a shift in stance was bound to force a rearrangement of the themes and emphases of the Catholic faith and identity experience. The pistic experience had to be freed from its unnecessary, entirely time-determined, anxious dependency on clericalism and clear boundaries; and in any case, it could no longer be the Catholic believer's normative experience.

## The Charismatic Experience

The single most significant reversal of ecclesiological perspective brought about by Vatican II is that the Church is not the Kingdom of God, but the sacrament of that Kingdom. In other words, the Church *mediates* between God and the world. This was bound to affect very deeply indeed the Church's relationships to the world, and hence, her style of evangelization.

A second reversal of perspective, and one hardly less significant, concerns the Catholic Church's relationship to the other Christian Churches and communities. Vatican II did not conceive the Catholic Church as simply identical with the Church of Christ. Rather, it taught that the Church of Christ "subsists in"[12] the Catholic Church, thus leaving room for the recognition of ecclesial reality in other Christian bodies. Again, this was bound to have far-reaching effects on the practice of ecumenism.

However, we would do well to reckon with the probability that it will take a long time for the Church at large to translate these new concepts into practice. One important reason for this expectation is the following. Catholics as a body, having traditionally relied so heavily on boundaries and definitions for their sense of identity, need a *deepening* of their identity experience. But now that the deepening has to occur while the Church is simultaneously exposed to an unprecedented *widening* of perspective and involvement, we can anticipate a long and often painful process. Catholics will have to work out their inner convictions, not in the comparably safe setting of a well-defined and well-defended Church, but in the *diaspora* of the real world.

Let us take just one example from the United States. James Hennessey wrote about the G.I. Bill of 1944, by which higher education suddenly came within the reach of thousands of Catholic World War II veterans: "One of the great levelling processes in American history was underway, and its effects were greatly felt among Roman Catholics."[13] The Catholic community became a confident[14] part of American society, and began to make significant contributions to it, and it did so from a position which it had not hitherto occupied: the increasingly well-educated, well-off center of American society. But for this position of influence and sophistication to be matched by an equally influential and sophisticated faith-commitment, major changes had to be in the offing. It is not without reason that Hennessey, having recounted the arrival of American Catholics in the mainstream of society, came to write the next and final chapter of his book under the title "A Revolutionary Moment."[15]

Changes are indeed occurring. Let us, for the moment, focus on some of the positive changes. The development programs for religious sisters in theology and religious education of the fifties and early sixties have blossomed into an explosion of theological endeavor which now involves not only sisters but also brothers and many priests, and increasingly large numbers of lay people, male and female. But behind and underneath this development of theology at the professional level, there is an even greater and deeper movement, namely, the emergence of ministerial practice and education among lay people and religious women and men. Watching the student populations of the various summer institutes in religious education and pastoral ministry is certainly very exhilarating, but it can also send shudders down one's spine. If all these perceptive, motivated, generous women and men should be frustrated, that would amount to a tragic failure on the part of the Catholic community to welcome the grace offered to it towards its own growth and development in faith.

The same thing can be said for the many informal "basic communities" that have arisen: prayer groups, Bible study groups, student ministry groups, and chaplaincies at colleges and universities, shelters for the homeless, therapeutic communities, groups for married couples and for divorced and single Catholics and friends—all of them organized for the purpose of mutual help and support and upbuilding.

Finally, there are the sizable groups that have adopted issues of public policy and social and international justice as their special concern: national and international injustice and poverty, racial and sexual discrimination, human life, peace and war, and disarmament—to mention only a few of the most important.

The changes enumerated here are occurring in the United States and Canada; but analogous developments are underway in Latin America, in Africa, in India, and Indonesia. Motivated Catholics are exercizing their baptismal privileges without being *authoritatively* directed by clergy on a habitual basis, and without benefit of formal ecclesiastical sanction and approval.

The rise of this new, or at least relatively new, type of believer cannot be entirely attributed to Vatican II. Its roots are in St. Pius X's call for frequent and even daily communion, in Pius XI's *Actio Catholica*, and in Pius XII's call for the laity's active participation in the liturgy as well as his consistent efforts to promote the christianization of professional life, witness his many addresses to professional societies. Still, there is no doubt that Vatican II did unleash a new type of Catholic identity-experience.

This book proposes to call this experience 'charismatic,' and it refers to people whose faith and identity experience is strongly characterized by the exercise of *charismata*, or gifts. Christians who are in this general category tend to be less dependent on ecclesiastical and clerical assurance and tradition. They are bent on leading lives of active virtue on the strength of a more personalized experience of faith. Hence they tend to manifest a desire to put themselves, along with their gifts, at the service of Church and world—or at least out in the open.[16]

This new type of Catholic faith-experience is, of course, not new in the sense of unprecedented. We have always had women and men of personal faith and virtue in our midst, and they were often content to suffer at the hands of the ecclesiastical establishment. But this type of person has become rather more numerous of late, and its main positive features are worth enumerating.

First of all, charismatics operate in the *diaspora*. They have, with Vatican II, opted in principle for an open Church, one that is *not primarily* defined by boundaries. Rather than staying within the confines of the pistic faith-experience, in a forensic, judgmental stance with regard to the world, charismatics tend towards *solidarity and communication*. They are intrigued by what is out there. They are keen on discovering the characteristics of the faith of Protestants. They take an interest in what is secular. To the seasoned observer, they are sometimes a bit naive, but it is impossible to doubt their sincerity. In countries where the Catholic Church continues to have strong political ties—usually only half-consciously, given the long tradition—the accusation is often heard that these "new Catholics" are immature, and that they involve themselves too much in politics. What *is* often the case is that the "new Catholics" are involved with groups and issues that have traditionally remained outside the sphere of interest of the politico-ecclesiastical establishment, with its experience in the practice of *Realpolitik*. This interest on the part of motivated Christians in neglected concerns in society at large, such as the poor, tends to make the establishment very uncomfortable.

Secondly, charismatic believers tend to be *actualists*, and they can point to many features in Vatican II to support their stance. Rather than just living by tradition, they tend to be motivated by the call of the moment, by the excitement as well as the distress they find in the situation in which they live. As a result, there tends to be a strong emphasis on immediate involvement and on the imitation of Christ, of the historical Jesus, as he moves around his contemporaries, available to all as a teacher, a healer, a challenger, an example, and a friend. Charismatics have a strong sense that faith, far from being a passive reception of a salvation vicariously wrought by Christ, is an active life of responsibility and involvement, and a quest for life rather than an assurance of it.

This leads to the third characteristic: charismatics are *personalists*. This shows up in a variety of ways. They are motivated, which tends to make them conscientious and resistant to general rules. They intentionally search for authenticity while often mildly agonizing about the hardships of the search. But they do not like to be reminded of the accumulated wisdom of the tradition. They like to be discretionary in their decisions; and they resent being told, dogmatically and didactically, what to believe and what to do. Vatican II's definition of the Church as "the People of God" and its emphasis on the common priesthood of the faithful came to them as a welcome, long overdue affirmation of their status as Christians and Catholics in their own right, and not just at the sufferance of the clergy. While it is foolish to deny that Vatican II unleashed a crisis of authority, it is equally foolish to deny that it unleashed a surge of *integrity, authenticity, and personal responsibility*.

This leads to the fourth characteristic. The movement just described was bound to create confusion and uncertainty as well as clarity and exhilaration. Deeper integration requires the experience of deeper conflicts; the discovery of a deeper faith-commitment is usually preceded and accompanied by deeper doubts. This in turn generates a greater need for experienced community around faith-issues, as well as the informal exercise of realistic, experience-based ministry by many persons in many ways. For if the pistic community is characterized by uniformity, the charismatic type is characterized by *pluriformity and differentiation of ministries*—which is our fourth characteristic, and again one of the themes of Vatican II. In the New Testament, the First Letter to the Corinthians functions both as the charter and as the critique of this kind of Church community.[17]

People working out a personal synthesis need to share, and so they seek out others with similar needs. The search tends to be contagious, and entire communities are affected by a funny mixture of excitement at the atmosphere of discovery and panic at the loss of the familiar patterns of coherence. The latter, in turn, tends to increase the felt need for ministry. More motivation among the faithful requires, paradoxically, more ministry, not less. And the ministry required must be the kind that is not so much authoritative as compassionate. "The Wounded Healer"[18] has become one of the favorite models of ministry.

Needless to say, all of this has brought enormous pressures to bear on the ordained ministry as well as on religious communities, especially those without orders. To begin with the latter, they used to take their direction largely from the clergy, and they largely viewed their work as accessory to the clergy's work. The recent rise of ministerial inspiration among the laity has faced them with a formidable challenge. Those among the religious who have been able to resist the attraction of the lay life seem to have gone in two directions. Some communities have battened down the hatches, pulled together, and emphasized the traditional stance. Most religious communities, however, seem to have increasingly taken their cue from the ministerial sensibilities developing among the motivated laity, and they have come to view the laity rather than the clergy as their natural allies. Many religious now refer to what they used to call their "work" as their "ministry," and rather than functioning as the "personnel" of the "institutional Church," they now tend to venture out among the faithful at large, offering and receiving fellowship, service, and inspiration in a great variety of ways.

The pressures on the ordained ministry have been no less dramatic. Priests were largely educated in an undifferentiated setting, and so tended to function best in a pistic church. But recently the developing ministries have started to test and question and challenge and to some extent erode the ordained ministry as well as the traditional, pistic community structure, which is so comfortable with clericalism. These developments have upset many in the Church, and it must be said that Paul's repeated call, again in I Corinthians, for love and concern for these weaker members of the community is of high relevance here.[19] But then again, so is his defense of the variety of gifts in the same letter. Pistics and charismatics, traditional ordained ministry and the new ministries will have to learn to live together and cooperate; and this is likely, eventually, to alter the shape of the Church community and its ordained ministry in significant ways.

For the time being, however, this involves an invitation extended to priests to enter more deeply into the experiences of the more motivated among the people they are called to serve, and *vice versa*. There is a need for growth in mutual trust, in the sharing of influence and responsibility, and even in affective relationships. This is in character with the nature of charismatic community: it tends to bring all kinds of different people into contact with one another at more personal levels. That this involves the risk of uncritical and immature responses should be as obvious as the fact that it affords real opportunities for personal and corporate growth for ordained ministers as well as for motivated laity. The past fifteen years have shown plenty of instances of both. But, then, pluralism surrounds us everywhere, much of it heartening, much of it vulgar, most of it wholesome. All of these influences are also liable to be felt in a community that tries to bring hearts and heads into a faith-enterprise which a previous generation largely experienced as an essentially static pattern of beliefs and practices to be taken for granted. The simple fact is that the Catholic community is moving, in some of its members more than others and in some places more noticeably than others, from being simply a pistic, popular Church, in the direction of being also a charismatic, motivational Church—that is to say, a Church with far better prospects for survival in a pluralistic society.

## Serious Questions

So far, this chapter has mainly concentrated on the positive aspects of the charismatic experience. It is time to mention and elaborate some of its inherent limitations and dangers. This will put us in a better position to raise the issue of identity again.

First of all, while there is no doubt that a stance of *solidarity and communication* is in keeping with the open-church theology adopted by Vatican II, the risk of *diffuseness and compromise* connected with this should not be underrated. This takes on different forms in different types of societies. In some, a vague liberalism is liable to extenuate the Catholic identity; in others, the danger of various forms of syncretism is not imaginary.

Wherever the Church finds itself in the diaspora of a *modern*, open, secular society, she will also feel the subtle impact of the tendency to level and equalize, which is the dark side of a prevailing atmosphere of toleration and civil liberty. Churches, in such situations, risk being measured principally by the yardstick of public relevance. One notable effect of this kind of measuring is ethical: there is pressure on the Church not to let her ethical demands exceed the reasonable and generally accepted demands of public morality.

Wherever the Church is in the diaspora of a *traditional* society (which is often the case in the Third World), she will feel the impact of other religions or quasi-religious groups, which very often are quite intolerant and put a lot of pressure on the community of believers. Churches, in such contexts, often find themselves tempted to purchase peace by means of syncretistic accommodation.

Secondly, the *actualism* of the charismatic stance may lead to a serious *loss of tradition*. The Church's great Tradition is a complex and delicate structure of considerable subtlety. Its riches and its profound coherence are not habitually realized by the pistic community, nor even by its leadership; for the pistic community tends to live and remember by habit and definition rather than by appreciation. The pistic community has the deposit of faith, the discipline of life, and the forms of worship largely, so to speak, under wraps or in boxes. It lives by possession and a sense of security rather than by enjoyment and a sense of wealth.

The community that moves in a charismatic direction tends to be excited at its own openness. It tends to view tradition as cumbersome and irrelevant and hardly applicable. It will appeal to "experience" to justify the manner and the substance of its involvement in the world at large. There is certainly much to be said for this. Still, what does *experience* mean? Philosophically, it happens to be one of the least clarified notions of the century. Often, in fact, *experience* is little more than a slogan to cloak a polemical rejection of whatever used to be intellectually established and authoritative. Hence, much of the liberalism advocated by charismatics must be called superficial. This does not mean that it is perverse; for it is not, in most cases, a willful rejection of the tradition. Rather, it lacks depth, born, as it often is, out of unfamiliarity and even ignorance. We are touching here on one of the recurring themes in Hans Urs von Balthasar's writings; he makes no secret of his horror at what he interprets as the casual abandonment of doctrines and practices of considerable depth in favor of more acceptable positions.[20]

Thirdly, another consequence of the charismatics' actualism is a fair amount of *dissipation* and even some mild, mostly unintentional heresy, with various groups citing their own favorite authorities.[21] This requires explanation. In the experience of many motivated Christians, quite a few features of the Christian tradition are irrelevant and foreign. This leads to a selective understanding and a selective acceptance of the tradition. In this way what is a positive good, namely a differentiated understanding of the faith and the willingness to exercise the great variety of gifts and ministries, turns into something negative: the pushing of a variety of agendas, often in a very competitive fashion. Anyone familiar with, say, a lively urban or suburban parish is aware of the difficulty involved in promoting understanding and mutual forbearance between motivated groups with very different priorities. Personal faith and integrity and authenticity are indeed essential, but they may not become the sole norms for what is valid in doctrine, ethics, and worship. One of the strengths of the personalist, charismatic stance is that charismatics *choose*. One of its weaknesses is that they tend to *select*, which means that they often reject what does not appeal to them, and even more often they practically consign it to oblivion. It would be foolish to deny that pluriformity harbors the risk of disintegration; and this is true not only for small-scale entities like parishes or dioceses, but even for the global Church.

This has consequences in the areas of ecumenism and evangelization. The charismatic stance is, of course, inherently open and in that sense ecumenical and evangelistic. And yet, it tends to be insufficiently aware of two serious problems. The first is a penchant for *ad hoc* doctrinal, ethical, and liturgical accomodations that suffer from lack of depth. The second is the factionalizing of the Church. There is no cause for excessive concern here, and we should certainly not allow fear to force a return to the rigid pistic structures of the past. Still in some places we *have* seen the rise of what has been called "third confessions"—quasi-independent communities somewhere in between traditional Catholicism and liberal Reformation. This amounts to a further division of the Christian community, a disastrous and profoundly unecumenical development.

Fourthly and finally, we must mention what is easily the most serious and menacing feature of the charismatic stance: the insidious tendency to adopt *a completely moralistic version of the Catholic faith and identity experience*. This must be elaborated.

One of the strengths of the charismatic experience is the grateful and appreciative discovery of personal faith, of active involvement in ministry as a personal call, and of productive talents to be well used. No wonder the charismatic is attracted to the life of the historical Jesus. But active involvement, especially when the charismatic's tendency to selectiveness is kept in mind, can turn into a questionable, self-righteous kind of self-affirmation, with a tendency towards factionalization and intolerance towards others in the Church. Factions, moreover, have a strong need for self-justification; they need to state a rationale to account for what they seek. The problem is that the rationale often takes the form of an attempt to cast Jesus in the role of an advocate of the faction's own cause. Eventually, Jesus is seen predominantly as a teacher, a prophetic advocate, an inspiring model for action, or even as a hero, a fighter, or a martyr—but interpretations like these move Christology in any real sense into the background.[22] In this way, the experience of Christian identity tends to be reduced to an experience of moral Ego-strength after the alleged example of Christ, often with an edge of self-righteousness. Christ tends to be quoted in justification of one's own behavior, while the mystery of his person tends to be reduced to the significance of his alleged cause.[23]

To the extent that this tendency persists, three serious dangers appear on the horizon.

First, the Catholic identity-experience, which must involve *membership in a community, tends to be reduced* to a sense of being part of a broad *movement* called Christianity. The question thus tends to become: what is so compelling about being a Roman Catholic? In the afterglow of Vatican II, advocacy of the "movement"-character of the Church seemed to be a good way to reduce the emphasis on "institution." The problem is, however, that movements afford little sense of identity, which is the only basis on which a tough-minded openness with real focus is possible. Heinrich Böll, with characteristic forthrightness, has pointed out that the habit of many open and ecumenical Catholics (and Protestants) to refer to themselves as "Christians" makes them sound rather vague and complacent.[24]

Secondly, the charismatics' turn to motivation and action may involve a *contempt of the weaker brothers and sisters* in the Church—those "for whom Christ died."[25] Charismatics tend to be "gnostics." To use the language of I Corinthians, they must be reminded of the "more excellent way"[26]—more excellent, that is, than all the charismata. That way is the life of *agape*, affectionate regard for the weaker brothers and sisters in the community.

Thirdly, the Christian identity-experience ceases to have a compelling center; *the person of Christ tends to lose its decisiveness*. Socrates, the Buddha, Mahatma Gandhi, and so many other great and generous souls have labored and are still laboring for a better world or for a higher humanity without the awkward claim to being the key to the universe. But such a posture takes the focus out of all evangelization.

## Pistics and Charismatics: Common Limitations

The second half of this chapter has concentrated on the charismatic faith and identity experience as opposed to the traditional, pistic experience. It would be a mistake, however, to create the impression that the two types of faith have little or nothing in common. The contrary is true: pistics and charismatics share a few important features. We must briefly take cognizance of this fact in the remainder of this chapter. Then we will be ready for the consideration of the third type of faith-experience, the mystical, which will be the main subject of the third chapter.

First of all, pistics and charismatics are both concerned with the past and the present; a future perspective does not loom large in their faith-experience. It is, of course, true that pistics do believe in the last things, and that charismatics very much yearn and struggle for a better world in the future; but neither take their cue from eschatology in any consistent fashion. The next chapter will argue that this is a real limitation of the pistic and charismatic stances, and one which must be corrected by a consistent application of eschatological perspective.

Secondly, we argued that the pistic stance, especially in the form in which it has come down to us, is excessively forensic and judgmental vis-a-vis the world.[27] It is important to observe, however, that the charismatic stance is no less judgmental. Not only are charismatics continually tempted to intolerance, but their very openness leaves them wide open to the covert judgmental activities of *permitting and condoning*. If pistics tend to condemn, charismatics tend to condone; but there is less difference between condemning and condoning than meets the eye. The arrogance of power lies at the root of both. To put the matter in psychological terms, the pistic may be blocked by dependency; the charismatic tends to be blocked by counterdependence. The pistic may be prejudiced; the charismatic tends to have a prejudice against all firm stances. This, incidentally, places authorities in the Church in an especially precarious position vis-a-vis the charismatics. Treating them as pistics, that is, summoning them to return within the boundaries, is more likely to cause alienation than compliance. Sermonizing them is likely to have no result. But in any case, both the pistic and the charismatic stance must find a deeper anchorage than judgment.

Thirdly, we argued that the pistic experience was kept structurally impatient and inhospitable.[28] How about patience and hospitality in the charismatic world? It has already been pointed out that the charismatic's impatience and inhospitality may be directed against fellow Church-members rather than outsiders. We might add that motivated Christians are often impatient and inhospitable with regard to themselves, too. They have a hard time accepting their own immature, compliant, pistic past. But is their attitude to the world and to other Christians not characterized by openness? Undoubtedly it is. And yet in all honesty we may ask the question: Is the charismatic stance really that patient, that hospitable? If everything goes, nothing makes any real difference. If everyone is welcome, nobody really is. When on one occasion, G. K. Chesterton heard a friend praise a common acquaintance to the skies on account of the latter's great openmindedness, he remarked that the mind of Mr. So-and-so was, in fact, so open that by now everything had dropped out of it. It takes a true sense of identity to be really patient, to let the pain of another person's estrangement really get to one. It takes a true home to open itself to receive guests, even difficult ones.

In our first chapter we argued that the faith-experience associated with boundaries, and hence the practice of ecumenism and evangelization as a function of negotiation, must not go unquestioned or unchallenged.[29] It must now be added that the faith-experience associated with common concerns, and hence the practice of ecumenism and evangelization as a function of present relevance, must not go unquestioned or unchallenged either. This is the same as saying that the charismatic attitude of openness is not the definitive answer to our questions about identity and openness. It fails to provide the kind of identity experience that *includes* openness as an integral part of itself.

By way of conclusion, let us go back to Vancouver. To judge by the preparatory documents, that Assembly seemed to be headed in a consistently charismatic direction. The main theme, "Jesus Christ—Life of the World," was elaborated in four sub-themes. What was striking was that the four sub-themes elaborated the main theme in terms of *causes*, four strongly ethical causes: (1) Life, a Gift of God; (2) Life Confronting and Overcoming Death; (3) Life in its Fullness; and (4) Life in Unity. The concerns behind these themes were clear: Christians are to witness in a divided world; they are to seek for ways towards unity; they must promote, against the powers that be, participation of people at large and emancipation of the world's poor; they must attempt to promote community and to heal broken community; they must serve the causes of peace and human survival, international justice and human rights; and they must communicate in such a way as to convey conviction.

One would have to be Philistine to quarrel with these themes; they are obviously absolutely vital. But many people noticed, in the preparatory documents, the absence of substantial references on the one hand to the so-called ordinary faithful, the pistics, in the Churches, and on the other hand to the practice of worship. Not surprisingly, there were those who were wondering whether the ethical, charismatic element in Vancouver was going to push aside the pistic and the mystic elements, much to the detriment of an integral sense of Christian community and identity and of the central place of Jesus Christ.

But what happened was something else. In the wake of the Lima Report, the central themes of Baptism, Eucharist, and Ministry came to take pride of place. And if the Vancouver Assembly came to be remembered for any single event, it was the common Eucharistic Liturgy.[30] Where two or three are together in his name, the Living Christ will surprise them, no matter how ethically serious they are. He will lead them to the invisible Father in worship, in the power of the Holy Spirit.

*THREE*

# Sharing Life:

## Mystical Identity in Patience and Hospitality

### Introduction: Universality, Eschatology, and Christ's Resurrection

Our first chapter explained that Vatican II came to deal in a prophetic manner with the fact that the Catholic Church is now for the first time in history actually faced with the challenge of becoming a global Church,[1] of becoming the Church Catholic, not only as a matter of principle, but also in the empirical order. That amounts to an enormous widening of horizons, in space as well as time. Never before has the Church been in a position to have a more realistic (and a more daunting!) appreciation of her universal mission, and never has her eschatological orientation directed her more compellingly to her responsibility for the future.

These two themes together, the demand for a truly universal Church and the call of a truly open future, are, in the New Testament, associated with the *Resurrection* of Jesus Christ, which makes available to all who believe access to God's glory and God's mercy, in the name of Jesus the living Lord.

In the ancient world where religion was identified with *particular* pursuits, places, nations, and political establishments (a stance which the later Church would not always be able to avoid), the Christian Gospel proclaimed that it was meant for all people to the very ends of the earth, regardless of race, social class, or sex. There was One who had been manifest in the flesh and who was now risen, that is to say, alive and vindicated in the Spirit and taken up in glory, having confronted the powers of the universe. He was also the One who was now being preached among all nations and accepted in faith by men and women everywhere.[2] The world, therefore, was no longer at the mercy of the powers that be, with their tendency to divide and conquer. Rather, it had been made whole and free, that is to say, it had been made universally accessible and acceptable in the Spirit of God.

Now for the first time, all the earth's nations were in a position to share the promises held out to Israel, as the prophets had foretold. Salvation had become a universal possibility. God was now revealed as the God who wishes to be worshiped and glorified by all, as the Savior who wants all of humanity to be saved and to come to the knowledge of the truth.[3] Welcoming one another in the one community without discrimination, therefore, had become an act of worship since it was an act of obedience to God's will for the world as revealed in Jesus Christ. His life of ministry in Israel had been the proof of God's *faithfulness* to his *chosen people*; but now that he was risen, he was also revealed as the long-expected gesture of God's *mercy* to *all nations*.[4]

And yet it was not only the entire *human* world that had been welcomed by God. Everything, "the earth and all that fills it," now had the opportunity of becoming effectively "the Lord's." Therefore, nothing would henceforth be incapable or unworthy, at least as a matter of principle, of being accepted with gratitude and thus being drawn into the sacrifice of praise and thanksgiving, to the glory of God.[5]

All of this, of course, amounted to the Church's undertaking a task of evangelization whose accomplishment was to have no limits. It was a task that could no longer be measured by the standards of the past, but only by the future and its unfinished agenda.

In this way, a totally new perspective on the *future* arose. As a matter of fact, the very use of the word *resurrection* to convey what God had done for Jesus betrayed this very perspective. The reason for this is that the word *resurrection* and the aspiration conveyed by it were themselves entirely eschatological.

It is of crucial importance to be very clear on this. The word *resurrection* was *not* a new word, chosen by the eye-witnesses and the first communities as an appropriate means to *describe* what had happened to Jesus. Quite the contrary. "Resurrection" had been a live *aspiration* for two or three centuries, and it was still alive among many of Jesus' contemporaries. It was especially current among Pharisees, and as such it was a powerful piece of "lay spirituality."[6] When, therefore, the first eye-witnesses found themselves face to face with the Jesus who had died and who was now alive in the spirit, *resurrection* was one of the obvious words for them to grasp at to convey the inexpressible.

The main element in the aspiration was the firm conviction that final justice was only to be expected from God. Human judgment is often unjust and in any case always fallible. Many good people suffer, and many evil people achieve wealth and happiness. In fact, there is the ominous recognition that it is precisely the just and the righteous who, simply by being just and righteous and god-fearing, evoke in the unjust that tendency to throw their weight around and to test just people's faith and their dedication to virtue.[7] Hence, in order for true justice to be done, God must vindicate those whom he acknowledges as his own; he will raise them up, out of the death which, in the eyes of the unjust, had sealed their unhappy fate. He will raise them, have them "stand up," come alive in his presence forever, an eternal proof of his justice and an everlasting condemnation of the ways of the evil.

In this way worse repression and more dreadful suffering can become, in the eyes of the believers in the "resurrection of the flesh," not a reason for unbelief, but rather a reason for greater hope and encouragement. The so-called apocalyptic writings in the Old Testament bear out this ineradicable faith in a just God. The theme is also found in many places in the New Testament, including Jesus' eschatological sayings and sermons in the synoptic Gospels. Yet nowhere more clearly than in the book of Revelation do New Testament Christians identify with this powerful piece of late-Jewish spirituality. The evils of the world as we know it will have to come to a paroxysm of violence. But behind it all is enthroned the righteous mercy of a faithful God, whose Day will come. On that day God will recognize his own. Their names, known only to God and contained in the Book of Life, to be opened by the Lamb, will be revealed. Meanwhile, life in the world remains a long and often thankless wait for justice and right judgment; but both will come. And so, "it is by your endurance that you will keep your lives," as you realize that "the sufferings of the present age are no match for the glory that is to be revealed" to you.[8]

The Christian community draws the assurance that that glory *will* indeed be revealed from the bold and heartfelt conviction that God raised Christ from the dead. That is to say, the Christian community enjoys an inner vision of God's eschatological glory as it has appeared in the face of the risen Christ. But if Christ has been raised, we have God's own assurance that we will be raised as well. Hence the Christian community's confident habit of giving glory to God by the loud confession, "Jesus is Lord!" Hence, too, its confident yearning for the final reckoning, which will also be the final celebration of God's mercy and faithfulness, a yearning conveyed by the prayer "*Marana tha*," "Our Lord, come!"[9]

Let us sum up this introductory section. The

Church's mission is an eschatological and universal one, and it takes its origin from the risen Christ. He is and remains the living source of the Spirit that will recreate the whole world and bring all the nations into the peace of God's Kingdom, and the Church must be his instrument in bringing this about.

These chapters so far have argued that Vatican II mandated a renewal of the church, and that we see many signs of it in many places. We must now, in this third chapter, add that this renewal, if it is to be authentically Christian, must go back to the original and abiding realization that Christ is alive and present in the Spirit, a realization found everywhere in the New Testament and one that remains the original source of all Christian faith and identity experience.[10]

More specifically, these chapters have endorsed Rahner's conviction that the Church after Vatican II is faced with the challenge of becoming a global Church. They have also argued that the renewal mandated by Vatican II involves the development of a fresh arrangement of the themes and emphases of the Catholic faith and identity experience. This new experience, it was added, must involve a new sense of identity as well as a new style of openness, both of them at a level more fundamental than the traditional pistic and the more recent charismatic stances have thus far allowed. This third chapter intends to argue that in these circumstances the Catholic Church and her members can make no real sense, either of their identity or of their mission, unless they go back to their abiding foundation: the risen Lord.

## The Risen Christ as the Mystical Source of Identity and Mission

It has become a commonplace to observe that the New Testament, especially the Synoptics and the fourth Gospel, "read" the life of the historical Jesus in the light of the Resurrection; no true christological recollection is available to the Church outside the context of the Resurrection. What holds for the New Testament recollections also holds for the doctrinal tradition that followed: the worshipful boldness that comes from the Resurrection supplies the grounds for the affirmation of Christ's divinity, the affirmation of the consubstantiality of the Logos Incarnate with the Father in godhead.[11]

These two points must be combined with two observations we made in the previous chapter to yield two conclusions. The two observations were the following. First, it was suggested that believers of the charismatic type tend to take their cue from present, actual situations, and that their favorite christological theme tends to be the ministry of the historical Jesus.[12] Secondly, it was also suggested that believers of the pistic type tend to take their cue from the authoritative past, and that their favorite christological theme tends to be the Incarnation.[13]

The conclusions to be drawn from all of this are the following.

First, the charismatic-pistic concern with the *ministry* of Jesus and with the *Incarnation* does not in and of itself furnish us with a reliable sense of Christian identity and openness. These will come about only if the appropriate response to Christ's Resurrection is discovered, to provide the charismatic-pistic stance with a deeper foundation. What is this appropriate response? The next section will argue that it is *worship*; worship is and remains the crucial and indispensable ingredient of any kind of Christian identity-experience. This means that Christian identity is fundamentally a matter of *mystical* experience.

Secondly, the charismatic-pistic tendency to take its cues from the *present* and the *past* does not in and of itself furnish us with a reliable sense of Christian openness and identity. That will come about only if, again, the appropriate response to Christ's Resurrection is discovered, to provide the charismatic-pistic stance with a firmer foundation. This appropriate response is *witness*. And witness is essentially determined, neither by the urgency of the present nor by the authority of the past, but only by the demand of the *future*. The last section of this chapter will argue that this makes Christian patience and hospitality into the principal ingredients of the practice of ecumenism and evangelization.

Before launching into an exploration of Christian worship and Christian witness, of Christian identity and Christian openness, however, two fundamental points must be made.

First, worship and witness must be *taken together* to embody the experience of Christian identity and openness. This *combination* is vital. Witness prevents worship from degenerating into meaningless religiosity practiced in a closed circle where the words "Lord, Lord!" are indeed heard, but the will of the Father is not done. Worship prevents witness from degenerating into fundamentalist propaganda in which the authoritarian assurance of the preacher and his Bible passages replace the appeal of the living Word of God.

Secondly, the deepest reason why worship and witness must be taken together lies in their common origin, which is the Risen Christ. *The person of Jesus Christ alive in the Spirit is the source of Christian identity-experience as well as the Christian experience of openness to the world*. This means that neither the profoundest traditional Christian liturgy, doctrine, or discipline nor the most urgent Christian cause can replace the living Christ who is "yesterday, today, and tomorrow," as the Easter (!) liturgy has it. This must be briefly elaborated.

Devotion to the Tradition is a prominent characteristic of the pistic stance. There is much of value there. The traditional liturgies, disciplines, and doctrines are the shape of the Church's faith and the abiding, dependable symbols of the faith of our fathers and mothers. And yet for all their beauty and authority (and, in some cases, infallibility), the elements that make up the great Tradition are not the definitive, but the *provisional* shape of the faith, and that shape is capable of change and rearrangement.[14] Their deep significance does not lie in their shape, which is conditioned by time and place, but in their ability to express and represent, symbolically, the Church's hopeful and worshipful surrender to God in the Spirit, in response to the risen Christ. This is why it is often correctly said that the doctrines need the setting of worship and the orientation to the eschaton in order to convey their true meaning. It is the same as saying that it is Christ alive in the Spirit who gives them their true meaning. Pistics need to be reminded of this, lest the person of Jesus Christ be obscured by traditions and devotions. They must be reminded that the Gospels are filled with attempts by the historical Jesus to point the religious people of his day beyond the Law and the laws, the Tradition and the traditions, to the living God.

Charismatics tend to stress the need for Christian involvement in serious and pressing concerns and causes. Again, there is much of value there. Involvement and service are the way to follow Christ in the circumstances of the present Church and the present world. But concerns, urgent as they are, are always *partial*; they tend, in and of themselves, to compete, to generate opponents, and even to make enemies. There is a tragic element in dedication: particular pursuits require earnestness, both about oneself and about the pursuit. Thus the very act of involvement bears in itself the seeds of alienation both from one's deeper self and from others not sharing the same pursuit. This is why it is often rightly said that causes need the setting of worship and the orientation to the eschaton in order to make a true contribution. Again, it is Christ alive in the Spirit of *agape* that gives them their true significance. Charismatics need to be reminded of this, lest the person of Jesus Christ be obscured by advocacy, self-righteousness, and intolerance. The Gospels are filled with efforts to "test" Jesus, to force him to take sides in the ideologies, causes, and concerns of the day, or to force him to add yet another cause—his own—to the welter of causes already competing for ascendancy. Jesus, however, always refuses to identify himself with any cause. His "cause" is the Kingdom of God; but that is not a cause in the same order with other causes, let alone in competition with them. Rather, the Kingdom of God places *all* causes in an eschatological perspective, and so it meets and tests and assays all causes and concerns. The only cause Jesus is totally identified with is the Kingdom of God. Thus he is, as Origen put it, the *autobasileia*, the Kingdom in person.[15]

Hence pistics as well as charismatics must learn to center their vision on Jesus Christ who is, *in person*, the ultimate warrant of identity as well as openness in the Church. This is not just a matter of sound doctrine or discipline, but of letting oneself be instructed in the school of the Gospels.

The centrality of Jesus in the Gospels is, of course, most obvious in the Resurrection appearances where it is unmistakeably the *person* Jesus Christ, alive and present in the Spirit, who is revealed by the Father as the first-fruits of the new world—he and nobody else. But the focus on the person of Christ alive in the early apostolic kerygma includes a concentration on the person of the historical Jesus; the Risen one is "this Jesus."[16]

Therefore, it is not surprising to see that the passion narratives concentrate with increasing intensity on Jesus. When everything has failed, it is no longer possible to miss the point: the suffering, crucified, dying Jesus is the focus of the story. There, at the point of death, abandoned by all but a few disconsolate followers, Jesus is revealed as who he is: "Son of God," "the Just one."[17]

This concentration on the person of Jesus is even apparent in the pre-Passion narratives. Throughout the story of the Galilean ministry it may seem possible to focus on Jesus' work and on his impact rather than on his person. Even when Jesus starts limiting his ministry to his disciples, attention can still be diverted from his person, although, at least in Mark, the disciples' increasing misunderstanding of Jesus' mission leads to a growing isolation of his person. But on closer inspection the underlying focus on Jesus is hard to miss, even in the accounts of Jesus' active ministry. His work of healing, prophecy, and teaching is, at heart, a ministry of *encounter*: people meet the embodiment of the Kingdom of God in the *person* of Jesus. The thesis that Christian identity is to be found nowhere apart from the person of Jesus Christ has excellent Synoptic credentials.

We stated that neither the tradition of the Church's doctrine, worship, and discipline, nor the urgency of the imitation of Christ in the concerns of actual life provide, in and of themselves, a secure basis for Christian identity; only the *person* of Christ does. By "the person of Christ" we are to understand, of course, the Lord Jesus, present and alive in the Spirit. He *draws* his Church and through her the whole world into his own worshipful abandon and surrender to God, his dear Father. At the same time he *communicates* his presence to his Church, a presence that must send her to the ends of the earth and to the end of time to continue his witness and to make disciples of all nations.[18]

Jesus Christ, the living Lord, in other words, unites in his person the themes of Christian identity and Christian mission. In the Resurrection his true identity is revealed: "Son of God in power in virtue of the Holy Spirit through his Resurrection from the dead."[19] But as such he is also, in the apocalyptic vision of John, "the faithful witness," who opens the present to God's eschatological future ("the first-born of the dead") and whose appeal and authority are universal ("ruler of kings on earth").[20] The entire fourth Gospel is based on the same theme: Jesus' identity can be established only with reference to the Father, with whom he is one and who sent him into the world—which is precisely what makes Jesus the authoritative (and indeed eschatological) witness to the Father's glory, graciousness, and truth.[21]

What we have in the person of Jesus Christ, therefore, is the coincidence of identity and openness, of encounter with God in the Spirit and mission to the world in the same Spirit. In Christ we see the original fullness of what is offered to the Church by way of grace and participation. There is a depth here that must not be traded away for anything. It must remain at the heart of all Christian faith-experience.

The Church has never been without witnesses to this mystical depth. We need only recall how St. Theresa of Lisieux, cloistered and all, made the simplest, deepest discovery of her identity and her mission at the end of years of inner struggle. She found that it was to be her personal vocation in the Church to practice Love, union with Christ and total self-giving for the Church's mission. What she discovered was that the two are radically inseparable. And if the leap between a saint and a theologian is in order, we may want to recall Johann Baptist Metz's recent interpretation of religious life in analogous terms as a way of practicing both "the mysticism and the politics of the imitation" of Christ.[22]

It is to the former of these two, the mysticism, that we must now turn.

## Worship as the Heart of the Mystical Experience

The decision of the Fathers of Vatican II during the early, very conflicted phase of the Council to concentrate on the reform of the liturgy was nothing short of providential. It confirmed, perhaps without full awareness of the import of this step, what people in the liturgical movement had been saying for almost a century, namely, that it is in the liturgy and in the life that feeds on the liturgy that the Church receives and celebrates, enacts and experiences her identity.

It had taken long years of trial and error, of action and reaction, and of devoted study and careful experiment to shape this deep-seated conviction, but take shape it did. Pius X reformed the Missal by giving the Sunday liturgies the precedence over Saints' feasts that they deserved. He restored Gregorian chant to its place of honor, and he called for frequent communion. Pius XII recognized the efforts of communities like the Benedictines of Solesmes in France and Beuron in Germany, and of men like Odo Casel, Romano Guardini, Pius Parsch, Joseph Andreas Jungmann, Lambert Beauduin, and Louis Bouyer in Europe, and of Martin Hellriegel, Gerald Ellard, and their associates in the United States (to mention only a few), by issuing his Encyclical *Mediator Dei* in 1947 and by starting the reform of the Holy Week Liturgy in the early fifties. In many places dialogue mass and a variety of other liturgical functions were being tried out. Vatican II did not start in a vacuum.

The Constitution on the Liturgy of Vatican II has tended to eclipse these early developments, especially *Mediator Dei*. In the case of this latter document, this is a pity, for its stark accuracy and its compelling definitions repay a rereading down to this day. On the very first page it states: "In every liturgical action, it is not only the Church that is present, but also her divine Founder. . . The Sacred Liturgy, therefore, is the public worship which our Savior, the Head of the Church, continuously offers to the heavenly Father, and which the community of Christian believers offers to her Founder and, through him, to the Eternal Father; to put it briefly, it is the entire complex of public worship of the mystical Body of Jesus Christ, that is to say, of its Head and its members."[23]

What *Mediator Dei* had stated as a principle, Vatican II began to carry out in practice. No wonder there was a lot of immaturity to start with, both during the Council and in the following decade. Many approaches to the renewal of the liturgy bore the imprint of the pistic concern with boundaries, rules, and rubrics, and of the charismatic concern with relevance. These approaches are far from dead, witness the many official and unofficial demands that the liturgy be celebrated exactly according to the letter of the texts and the rubrics laid down in the official documents, and the persistent practice of free experimentation in the interests of local relevance.

Rules and relevance, we should recognize, are not of superficial importance, even though they are not the ultimate in liturgical matters either. There is always a tension between them, and that tension has deep roots. In recent years anthropologists have insisted with renewed emphasis that the meaning of our lives, both individually and socially, is largely lodged in patterns ("structures") of observances that existed before we were around and which continue to form the symbolic framework of our own sense of identity and of our communication with others. Rituals, including ritualized language, are examples of such patterns. Precisely because of this symbolic significance of rites, changes in ritual tend to be very slow. Originality is costly, and when it occurs, it has an extremely unsettling effect, both on its advocates and its opponents. When the new liturgy was introduced, this was often done in an authoritarian fashion. The widespread, unofficial departures from the norms were often hardly less authoritarian. Both were largely unaware of the depths of feeling and meaning associated with ritual and its renewal. Over the past few years a relative calm seems to have settled in. The new liturgy has met with general acceptance, and in many places a quiet practice has developed of celebrating the liturgy in special ways, in spite of the fact that the forms in which this is done are often officially unauthorized.

Still, neither the acceptance of the renewed liturgy nor the continuing practice of free (and fairly responsible) experimentation deal with the main issue, stated so affirmatively by *Mediator Dei* and elaborated at such great length by Vatican II's Constitution on the Liturgy, *Sacrosanctum Concilium*. The roots of the liturgy go to levels deeper than stability or relevance, to where its fundamental dimension, that is to say, its *mystical* depth, is found.

In virtue of Christ's Resurrection and the gift of the

Spirit, the Church, gathered in response to the presence of the Risen Lord, is made to share in his *worship* of the Father. Worshiping God is no longer just a matter of groping or trying, but of Spirited assurance and boldness. God, the Father of Jesus Christ, enables his Church, by the gift of the Spirit, to praise him the way God deserves to be praised, and in a manner that does complete justice to God, namely, by appealing to Jesus ("in the Name of Jesus"). So when the Church praises God through Christ alive in the Spirit, she is truly acknowledging the living God. Both God's effective presence and the ability to respond to it have been granted to the Church in the Risen Christ. And the only adequate response to the presence of the living God is this: praise and thanksgiving.[24]

There are, in all of this, three elements that require our special attention.

The first is *awe*. For the Church to praise God the way God deserves to be praised is something that never turns into a matter of course. Hence the Church must live in awe at the Alleluia she hears herself sing; she must never take the gift of the Spirit for granted.

The second is *hope*. The Church's praise of God transports her, at least in signs and symbols, to the eschaton. Hence it is yearning that gives the Church's praise of God in the world its depth. Her present worship anticipates the eschatological praise in the new heaven and the new earth. The audible and gestural praises of the visible Church must be, for the interim, the physical basis of her spiritual worship, the earthen vessels in which the heavenly treasure is—ever so precariously—kept.[25]

The third is *the gift of identity*. The Church's true life is hidden with Christ in God. Thus she is truly at home with God, and therefore she deeply knows who she is with a knowledge that remains a gift and never turns into the Church's possession. This means that the Church's sense of identity is an *ecstatic* sense of identity, of the kind that is received in the very act of total abandon and surrender, and born out of an act of casting all cares and anxieties on God. That sense of identity is what she must communicate to all her members, too, and the sweeping titles used in the New Testament are simply overstatements that should lead the Church and her members to where awed silence and ineffable joy in the Holy Spirit come together: Temple and Household of the living God, Children of God, Beloved of God; Bride of Christ and Body of Christ, his Brothers and Sisters, and his Friends; a soaring Temple of the Spirit, built up from living Stones, and even with each member individually being a Temple of the Spirit, too; Communion of the Saints. The Blessed Virgin Mary, completely abandoning herself to God and thus bearing Christ out of the fullness of the Holy Spirit, is the most eloquent model of this sense of identity, and hence the model of the Church *par excellence.*[26]

Hans Urs von Balthasar has reminded us of a usage that starts with Origen and continues well into the Middle Ages. It refers to Christians who have notably dispossessed themselves and abandoned themselves to God as men and women with an *anima ecclesiastica*—a soul bearing the form of the Church.[27] Such inner abandon allows them to undertake a life devoted to others ("being-for-one-another") and to make their cares and concerns their own. Such people have a true, inner, mystical affinity with the Church. They recognize the Church wherever she is to be found with the joy and the gratitude that only deep recognition can give. The inner witness of the Holy Spirit has so transformed their sense of themselves that they recognize and stand in awe of the presence of the Spirit wherever it encounters them. They know what it means to live, by grace, at the point where the love of God and the love of the Church coincide. Prayer and worship are the heart of that knowledge.

The Church, therefore, must treasure the liturgy and keep it deeply alive, as the summit to which all "the Church's activity is directed" and "the fountain from which all her power flows."[28] Keeping the liturgy alive means, of course, keeping the *Spirit* of the liturgy alive—there lies the guarantee of the Church's identity.

This identity is most pregnantly actualized in the Eucharist. The heart of what the Church is all about (the *res sacramenti*, as the Scholastics would say) is the worshipful communion, through and with and in Christ present and alive in the Spirit, with the Father. In the mystical dimension of this Sacrament the Church comes to full actuality, as do those Christians who have found there both themselves and God.

We are dealing here with the mystical core of the Christian faith and identity experience. It is the gift of the Spirit who grants to Christians access to the depths of God through their participation in the mind of Christ.[29] If, therefore, the Church were to limit the options of her members to the pistic and charismatic stances, she would lose her soul, and Christ's Resurrection would be in vain.

But she would also lose her unity. Why? The pistic community, given its stance of dependency, is held together largely by the symbols of authority and external controls. And yet it derives its necessary *growth* largely from the ministry of the charismatics. But the charismatics, in turn, given their propensity for self-affirmation and dissipation, require the unobtrusive yet urgent call of the mystic to stay together. Only the ecstasy of worship and abandon and the dark night of the Cross of Christ will ultimately heal both the charismatic and the pistic from the incomplete sense of identity that comes from preoccupation with self. The mystic leads the Church to trust the deeper source of unity: One Father, one Lord, one Holy Spirit—Triune Source of the varieties of energies, services, and gifts.[30]

In this way, finally, the Church's real identity lies in the unity which coincides with her holiness. No one owns the Church; Christ ransomed her. Exercising influence in the Church always involves the risk of trespass and lack of awe. The pistic tends to see unity and holiness in terms of limitation, by means of enforcement of stability and boundaries. The charismatic tends to view them in terms of expansion, by means of commitment to action and openness. Both are man-made, that is to say, useful and even sacramental; but they do not in and of themselves carry the guarantee of the Spirit. The pistic tends to quench the Spirit and to despise prophecy. The charismatic tends to let a lot of things go untested. Only the mystic knows God, that is to say, he or she desires to be known by God, and so he or she loves.[31]

## Conclusion: Cultivation of Mysticism

It is time to draw some conclusions from this section. We will concentrate on three points, all of them concerned with the mystical dimension of the Christian life. The first two will deal with sources of Catholic identity, while the third will widen the horizon to include ecumenism and evangelization.

First of all, the Catholic faith and identity experience after Vatican II stands to gain decisively from *liturgical spirituality*. The emphasis on spirituality is important here. The benefits of the renewed liturgy are obvious, but we still run the danger of contenting ourselves with renewal at the pistic and charismatic levels: better understanding of the faith through the use of better liturgy as the fundamental instrument of catechesis, more sense of community and wider participation, liturgical celebrations focused on public issues, and so forth. Still, better understanding of doctrine and more appropriate moral exhortation do not add up to *prayer*. The single most dangerous threat to the new liturgy, whether of the authorized or the experimental variety, is *prayerlessness*. This is not a theoretical observation, but a practical one. Prayerlessness in the liturgy, in fact, is so widespread as to be almost taken for granted.

One example is the ordinary practice of celebrating the Eucharist. Prayerlessness at mass is not only found in the fact that the invitations to prayer ("Let us pray"), are usually followed by an inconsequential pause, which raises doubts as to whether the celebrant has heard his own call. It also occurs in the other prayers and in the eucharistic prayer itself, which are regularly recited in far too routine and uninspired a fashion,[32] or which, if improvised, tend to be so *ad hoc* and so loaded with special pleading as to sound like oblique sermons rather than prayers. It also applies to the sermon, which is mostly either instructional or exhortational in tone and content, much to the detriment of its *mystagogical* function. Preaching must bring us to awe and prayer, too. It is an integral part of good liturgical practice to regularly have sermons that are neither explanatory nor immediately relevant, but deeply contemplative and conducive to mature prayer: about the presence of God, the life that lasts, the surrender of love, the beauty of the earth, the privilege of faith, the darkness of much prayer, God as a difficult friend, the humanity of Christ, the love of neighbor and enemy, the ugliness of sin and violence, the yearning that makes the heart deep, the "little virtue of hope" (Charles Péguy), and the irresistibility of the suffering Jesus.

Secondly, in light of what has just been explained, the widespread *search for prayer, spirituality, and spiritual direction* among motivated Catholics over the past ten or fifteen years deserves to be viewed as a most significant development. Many "charismatic" communities and associations, and many Catholics involved, individually or in groups, in forms of "charismatic" ministry have recognized the need for prayer, and perhaps even more importantly, for *discernment.* Prayer and worship, in which we find access to the living God, are the source of Christian identity. But discernment is needed to sort out and test the ways in which we seek this access to the living God as well as the ways in which we seek access to the center of ourselves, where the issue of our deepest identity is settled. The liturgy employs and needs the confident, vocal praise of God as well as the awed sense of a mystery that inspires deep silence. After all, we celebrate the Presence of him who is among us, but he is also the Absent one, who has gone away to prepare a place for us.[33] Analogously, non-liturgical prayer employs and needs both the expressive exuberance of the charismatic prayer groups *and* the seemingly agnostic silence of those among us whose inner (and often somewhat pained) sense of mystery is more aware of the inadequacy of words than of their power of expression.[34] Both seek God, which is essentially a mystical pursuit, albeit carried out in less than entirely mature ways. Hence both need spiritual discernment to find the way and to guard against illusion.

Thirdly, *ecumenism and evangelization are, at heart, a mystical venture*. It takes an *anima ecclesiastica* to recognize a Christian or a community of Christians. Ecumenism is only safe in the hands of those Christians and those Churches that live out of a fundamental Christian mysticism. Only out of mysticism comes that spiritual affinity with other Christians that is the source of awe, hope and yearning, and secure identity. Such Churches and such Christians do not, of course, cease to be beset by human limitations and all-too-human sins. But this does not depress and embarrass them to the point of unbelief. All Churches need mystics to heal the scandal caused by their own sins and divisions, and as reminders to all that Jesus Christ, as well as their own deepest identity, can be found alive in the Spirit to the glory of God. Mystics are realistic and humble about themselves as well as about the Church: they are where they are and who they are because they find God. This also gives them an inner appreciation of the fundamental faith-experience of other Christians, not to mention an inner appreciation of the fundamental integrity of non-Christians. Mystics are not the slaves of their own Churches' boundaries, limitations, and sins either, although they suffer from all of them. And, while suffering from unnecessary limits and sinful divisions, they do not affect the kind of openness that takes existing distinctions and sinful divisions lightly.

All of this amounts to saying that sensitivity to a Church's holiness is a *sine qua non* for all ecumenical endeavor, including ecumenism at the pistic and charismatic levels. All too often the loud protestations that only God can bring about the unity of the Churches have a hollow ring to them. The same can be said for the "liberal" protestations that imply that the churches, underneath all their "superficial" differences, are "really" one. The Church's true unity coincides with her *holiness*, and only those who seek out the holy can expect to find the kind of unity that can give a divine soul to denominational diversity as well as to ecumenical openness. And this soul is the Spirit, in whom the Father and the Son are present to the Church.

For the time being, much ecumenism suffers from lack of mysticism. At the same time, there are signs of hope: the theme of worship and holiness is breaking through. The preparatory agenda of the World Council of Churches General Assembly at Vancouver was disappointing because of its deficient treatment of worship. There was plenty of active charisma, but also a certain lack of depth, and there was reason to wonder how relevant the proposed agenda was to the countless local congregations of pistic Christians for whom Sunday worship is closer to home and closer to God than charismatic denunciations of the multinationals and their evil ways. But then came the actual Assembly with its endorsement of the Lima statement and its common Eucharist: worship became the center!

In the same way, even the most promising conversations between the Catholic Church and other Churches, like the ones with the Anglicans and the Lutherans, keep on sounding, at least in part, like negotiations waiting for concessions rather than accounts of meetings seeking common worship. The guarded reception accorded to promising conversation reports by some central authorities in the Catholic Church[35] has been badly lacking in that tone of thankfulness and eschatological joy and that quality of yearning which comes from familiarity with God and the recognition of brothers and sisters in Christ. It is not without significance, therefore, that Cardinal Willebrands, in a 1982 address, has reminded us again that ecumenism must not content itself with "an agreement on certain doctrinal positions leading perhaps to a facile intercommunion" or with "simply [. . .] acting together." It demands nothing short of "communion in the faith and sacraments"—that is to say, worship: "being together as a communion in the name of Christ and in the power of his Passover."[36] And he added that "the unity of those who believe in Christ is not at all a domestic affair," but that it can be understood "only in relation to God's design for the whole of humanity." Sharing life in the community, in other words, is only the mystical inside of sharing life with the world at large. True, that is to say mystical, Christian identity involves universal openness as an integral part of itself. It is to that openness that we must now turn.

## Openness in Patience and Hospitality

If worship is at the heart of the Church, so is witness; the two are inseparable. As we pointed out above,[37] worship without witness gets separated from the world and turns into an act of tribal religiosity; witness without worship loses touch with God and turns into proselytizing and party propaganda. Thus the Church's worship is not compelling if it is not public, for all to hear; the Church's witness is not compelling, unless she is *over*heard to praise God in the Name of Jesus.[38] The Church's openness, in other words, is intrinsically connected with her identity. This proposition bears closer inspection.

The *shape* of the Church's worship is *narrative*: God is praised by the thankful recounting of the life and the death and the Resurrection of Jesus.[39] But there are two elements in this narrative worship that must be stressed: its *auto*biographical character and its orientation to the future. Let us start with the former.

*The narrative of Jesus' life, death, and Resurrection is the expression of the Church's own identity*; it is "testimonial autobiography." Two comparisons may serve to clarify this. A scholar or a musician, when asked to give an account of himself, is likely to pay tribute to a revered teacher. A husband or wife, when giving expression to his or her happiness, is liable to give a glowing account of his or her spouse. Analogously, the Church expresses her own identity by singing the story of Jesus Christ in order to worship God. This self-expressive song of praise is prompted by the *risen* Christ, and the risen Christ is the actualization of an eschatological aspiration. Hence *the Church's worship commits her to the world and the future*—which is the second element just mentioned.

What is really involved here is nothing other than the imitation of Christ. The risen Christ, we have argued,[40] is the source of the Church's identity. We must now elaborate that he is the source of her mission as well.

In the act of praising the Father by recounting the life, death, and Resurrection of Jesus, the Church commits herself to the imitation of him whose story she recounts. Thus the Church in her very worship pledges to follow Christ into the world and into the future where he has gone before her. There, at the end of the earth and at the end of time, he is waiting for the Church as well as for the whole world to come to him. The *power* of the Church's commitment to the imitation of Christ is the Spirit of the Risen One, given to her as the pledge of eternal life. The *model* for the Church's life of discipleship comes from Jesus' past example. The Church must now do what Jesus did. She is to be the herald and the embodiment of God's Kingdom; meet the world as it comes to her out of God's hand, and never dismiss it; not please herself, but do the will of the Father, who sent Jesus, who in turn sends her; accept in trust what the Father entrusted to Christ; make every effort to let nothing and nobody get lost; hold out the promise of the Resurrection; represent the Son for all to see.[41]

The Church is called to be and do and teach all of this in expectation of and in deference to Christ's truthful and merciful judgment to come. This will give her the freedom and the carefreeness to act. Since her identity is a gift given to her gratuitously and not the product of self-constitution, the Church must learn to be basically unworried about her mission. She must learn how to give of herself without self-consciousness, self-maintenance, or self-justification. She is to follow Christ in not judging the world, but in being the agent of its salvation. Likewise, she is to follow him in not seeking her own glory. She is always tempted to seek her own glory in the interest of seeking some worldly security. She may, for instance, claim Jesus Christ as *her* Savior in order to establish or maintain her own identity *over against* the world; or she may attempt to justify herself and her own decisions by setting herself up as her own judge, thus refusing to stand under the judgment to come.[42] But the imitation of Christ is neither in condemning nor in condoning. It is in seeking God above all things, and thus to meet the world. It is essential, therefore, to insist on *encounter*—or, as the late Pope Paul VI loved to put it, *dialogue*—as the essential dynamic by which the Church in imitation of Christ must meet the world.

This means that it is wrong to characterize the Church's task simply in terms of activity or passivity, of activism or compliance. The Church's mission is bound to be a ministry of *action*, as was Jesus' ministry. The problem is that action is always liable to be undertaken in the interest of establishing one's own identity *over against* the object of the action. We tend to draw a firm line around us, whether individually or as a group, usually appealing to the weight of rights and truths established by precedent, and then proceed to deal with the forces we find in the outside world in order to establish ourselves, to our own satisfaction, as an influence to be reckoned with. In this fashion action is always tempted to degenerate into use, domination, and even exploitation. In action, in and of itself, there is a latent tendency to violence. The power to act, therefore, is only safe in our hands to the extent that our faith and identity experience is not a matter of self-assertion, and thus, to the extent that we are able to act on empathy and on inner affinity with the things or the persons we deal with, that is to say, secure enough not to have to hide behind protective barriers. Hence it is always good to bear in mind the passage in Matthew's gospel where Jesus' *active* ministry of healing and exorcism is presented as the fulfillment of Isaiah's prophecy about the *compassionate*, suffering servant of God, open and vulnerable and undefended.[43]

The pistic Church, well-defined as it is, is indeed poised for action; but since the test of action in imitation of Christ is compassion, she must always be ready to examine her conscience on this score. In her dealings with other Churches and the world at large, the Church must indeed protect her identity as well as the faith of her weaker members to some extent by means of definition and boundary, especially in critical situations. But when she does so, her mission does not cease to put her under an obligation to seek to understand actively what it is that moves the other Churches and the world. The pistic stance, while deserving special respect and care,[44] must not be made into the normative stance. Impassive resistance to passion and change is not a Christian virtue, nor is anxious dependence on ecclesiastical assurance. Both the Church and all its members are called to a life of openness and of action tempered by compassion.

However, if the Church must be open to the other Churches and to the world, that does not require her to purchase broad acceptance by means of conformity. If the pistic Church's temptation is in the direction of self-justification by means of active self-definition *over against* the outside world, the charismatic Church is tempted to justify itself by *being uncritically and passively open* to whatever comes along. Different images come to mind to convey the differences, as well as the basic problem. The pistic Church tries to be rich by hoarding, while the charismatic Church seeks wealth by indiscriminate buying; both are reluctant to embrace poverty of the spirit. The pistic Church tends to be immobilized by the weight of the past, while the charismatic Church tends to be impressed and weighed down by the welter of causes, ideologies, and concerns of the present; but both are afraid of the call of the future. Distressed by the narrow confines of the pistic Church, the charismatic Church lets herself be attracted by a variety of causes, and thus tends to get divided and scattered. Afraid of all that impinges on her, she tends to fear the judgment of all the tribunals that surround her, and to seek—always in vain—to find identity by pleasing the powers that be. If the pistic Church is tempted to be her own judge, the charismatic Church tends to defer to the judgments of the world, thus forfeiting the independence that comes from the confession of Jesus as Lord and coming Judge and the *imitatio Christi* that develops out of that confession.[45] The openness of the charismatic stance needs to be toughened by endurance, just as the closed ranks of the pistic stance need to be tempered by compassion.

Both the pistic concern with identity by self-preservation and the charismatic concern with identity by compliance have this in common, that they are *impatient and inhospitable*.[46] Afraid of the challenges that come from the outside, both pistics and charismatics reach, impatiently, for authoritative answers readily available. They give in to the urge towards self-maintenance, whether by rigidity or by spinelessness. In this way they pass up the opportunity to show their identity by the practice of patient flexibility. Embarrassed by the awkward void created by the meeting with the stranger from the outside, both the pistic and the charismatic, eager to show off the wealth of their resources, avoid a real dialogue; no true welcome is extended. The pistic will quote the authoritative answers from the past, and the charismatic will recite the latest line, but neither will make it a point to get to know the stranger. But for a traveler looking for a place to stay, there is little difference between closed doors and no home at all. Jesus was open to all, yet he did not defer to anyone. He chose the way of compassion and endurance, of patient, persistent encounter, and he offered the kind of welcome that only the poor in spirit can extend.

Only a deep sense of identity—that is to say, only worship—can enable the Church to desire to be so deeply patient and hospitable.[47] This applies not only to the Church's relationships with other Churches and the non-Christian world; *it also applies to the community of the Church itself.*

A Church that lives out of worship will be patient and hospitable *ad intra*, too. It will, in other words, cultivate active, appreciative, and even creative tolerance of ambiguity and differences. To put this in the terms used in the first chapter of this book: patience and hospitality must go into the shaping of a new, more flexible arrangement of the themes and emphases of the Catholic Church's faith and identity experience. The unity-in-pluriformity advocated by Vatican II is at heart a matter of worship, because only worship can generate the confidence and the mutual trust needed for *communion seen as an active process*. Even the best and most up-to-date rubrics, rules, and doctrinal definitions will produce nothing more than uniformity if they are not set in the context of worship and of active, perceptive, patient, confident communication.

This means that the Catholic Church must *seek* to be a Church in dialogue with herself, just as she must be in dialogue with the other Churches and with the world. The Catholic Church is faced with the challenge to become a global Church, and in the same process she is being invited, by inner developments, to enter upon a new experience of identity. This means that she must face the issue of *integrity:* the *style* of the Church's dealing with the outside world must be compatible with the way she practices *communio* inside. If openness is simply and unavoidably *thrust* on a Church unfalteringly committed to a traditional self-image with strongly political overtones, no dialogue will ensue, but only negotiation across boundaries far too firmly fixed.[48] If the profession of faith demanded of Catholics continues to make the pistic experience normative and remains dutifully tied to the exaggerated definitions of the past, then no deeper sense of identity will ensue, but serious loss of commitment, as well as lip-service to things recognized as unnecessary and even untrue.[49]

This little book is not the place to elaborate this. It would take many pages to apply the patience-and-hospitality theme to the three areas—teaching, life, and worship—in which the Church's identity as well as her openness to other Churches and to the non-Christian world must take place. An adequate treatment of the problem would also have to include an elaboration of the theme of patience and hospitality in a *spatial* sense and in a *temporal* sense. The Church must be a *global* Communion of communions, based on mutual trust and understanding, which in turn are inspired by worship and the call to global witness. The Church must also be a *historic* Tradition of traditions interpreted by means of a hermeneutic predicated on an appreciative attitude towards the varieties of history, which in turn is again inspired by the tradition of worship and witness.[50]

It is time to end. Could it be that there is Providence in the fact that the Liturgical Movement, the Ecumenical Movement, the globalization of awareness, and the development of modern communications media all go back to the years between, say, 1860 and 1900? Could it be that our rediscovery of worship has everything to do with the Church's Holiness, that our discovery of ecumenism has everything to do with the Church's Unity, and that our culture of globalization and communication has a lot to contribute to the kind of Catholicity that is not based on the glorification of boundaries? And could it be that the three are so deeply connected with one another that the Church, for the sake of her Apostolicity, should once again recognize the Stranger on the distant shore and, with Peter, jump into the water?

## APPENDIX ONE

# Three Levels of Faith-Experience

The threefold division proposed in this book represents an attempt to give a theological interpretation of some of the aftereffects of the second Vatican Council. These aftereffects occurred mainly in two areas: a renewal of church structures and an awakening of many of the faithful to a more personal experience of their faith.

Vatican II gave rise to a long overdue flourishing of *ecclesiology* in the Catholic Church. It concentrated largely on the New Testament origins of the Church and on the implications of the "People of God" theme for the structure of the Church; freedom and authority were some of its favorite themes. Among the names of authors that come to mind are, of course, Hans Küng and Richard McBrien. It must be added, though, that much in these explorations is concerned with the ecclesiastico-political rather than the mystico-theological features of the Church.

Another fruit of recent years, not only in the Catholic Church, but also in other Churches, is the attention given to the question of *faith-development*. It must be added, however, that the issue has been mainly approached from the point of view of developmental psychology so far, by thinkers like Erik Erikson, James Fowler, Sam Keen, William Rogers, and John McDargh. While the approach is obviously fruitful, it sometimes creates the impression that growth in the spirit is a function of human perfection. Hence it would seem that the complementary view, namely, that growth in the spirit is a matter of grace and finds its ultimate focus in God, needs to be stressed.

The *theological* approach advocated in this book goes back to some old traditions in ecclesiology and faith-development. The author is not qualified to present a full treatment. What this Appendix provides is no more than a coherent set of suggestions about the subject.

The first theme to come to mind is Clement of Alexandria's sequence *Protreptikos-Paidagogos-Didaskalos*: (Christ) "the Admonisher, the Tutor, the Master" (we can leave aside the question whether the *Stromateis* are, in part or in whole, identical with the *Didaskalos* or not). One difference is that the present book uses the word *mystic* instead of Clement's *gnostic*, which is liable to be misunderstood.[1]

We can also think of Origen's three-tiered theory on the interpretation of Scripture: the simple faithful must be instructed in the literal sense, those eager to practice virtue must find the moral sense, while those who are united with God seek out the spiritual (mystical, anagogical) sense. The terminology as well as the application of this triad was to go through many modifications, especially at the hands of Gregory the Great and the twelfth-century commentators on Scripture. Occasionally, a fourth sense was added. Deep down, however, the tradition remained true to itself, as Peter Lombard's summation of his own position indicates: "The historical sense is easier, the moral sweeter, the mystical sharper; the historical is for beginners, the moral for the advanced, the mystical for the perfect."[2]

The tradition about the three ways in the practice

of asceticism could also be alleged to support my division: the pistic's stance corresponds with the *via purgativa*, the charismatic is in the *via illuminativa*, while the mystic dwells in the *via unitiva*. There is a medieval commonplace that points in the same direction: a beginner in the faith should have his own salvation primarily at heart; someone who is advancing can learn how to be concerned with others in the practice of virtue; those who are advanced can afford, without fear of illusion, to focus their attention entirely on God.[3]

There is an interesting article by Pieter Smulders, S. J., which lays out the structure of the sacraments in an analogous manner: objective, publicly recognized Church membership in good standing is the basic level, upon which is built a life of active participation in the saving work of Christ the Mediator; the culmination of sacramental activity is the mystical communion with the Father in the Holy Spirit.[4]

I have come to think that my conception of the triple rhetoric in Christology (inclusion/Incarnation—obedience/humiliation—hope/Resurrection) is another way of dealing with the same basic issue. The simple faithful tend to be most impressed with the first—the fact that God became man for our salvation. Motivated believers tend to focus on the second—the historical Jesus and the call to discipleship. Persons who have the gift of interior prayer tend to take their cue from the Resurrection—the Presence of the God in Christ alive and present in the Spirit, experienced as the assurance of our access to the living God.[5]

I have also wondered on occasion whether the *triplex via* tradition (*via affirmationis, via negationis, via eminentiae*) could not be used to clarify levels of faith-experience. The pistic stance tends to be simply, and in that sense naively, affirmative about God. Charismatics have a more critical, reflective conception of God, owing to the fact that the experience of doubt is part of their makeup; hence they tend to regard strong affirmations about God with some suspicion and to stress the negative elements. Mystics can be most assertive as well as most apophatic, since they deeply recognize God's supereminence.

Finally, the three main forms of social relatedness (*Herde, Gesellschaft, Gemeinschaft*: herd, society, community), as explained, for example, in Max Scheler's *Wesen und Formen der Sympathie*,[6] have influenced my thinking on this subject.

The significance, as I see it, of the whole division is twofold. On the one hand, as indicated, I find the political and psychological approaches insufficient; they must be complemented by a theological interpretation of the issue. On the other hand, it is absolutely essential for the institutional Church to learn how to deal with the fact that not all Catholics live at the same basic level of personal and religious maturity—which is what I mean by saying that the pistic stance must no longer be assumed to be in a normative position.

I must, of course, apologize for the inelegant term *pistic*, which is far from euphonious. But I could find no better term, and it carries at least some weight on account of tradition.

*APPENDIX TWO*

# Two Examples

The third chapter of this book suggested that the style in which the Catholic Church should deal with the outside world must be compatible with her style in dealing with questions on the inside.[1] This Appendix offers a brief discussion of two examples in the area of *doctrine*. Both deal with the Catholic Church's relationships to the outside, the first in the area of evangelization, the second in the area of ecumenism. Both subjects are intimately related to the Catholic Church's identity-experience.

The first example is provided by Karl Rahner's repeated plea in recent years for the development of a number of *Kurzformel* or Brief Statements of the Faith.[2] The second example is provided by the first response of the Sacred Congregation for the Doctrine of the Faith to the *Final Report* of the first Anglican-Roman Catholic International Commission (ARCIC).[3]

## Rahner's Proposal for Brief Statements of the Faith

An introductory remark. If the Church's identity must include openness as an integral part of itself, then the doctrinal expressions of her faith and identity must be inspired by an attitude of *vicariousness*. "Vicariousness," in this context, means that the Church must think and feel, not only in her own behalf, but also in behalf of the world outside her. This requires that the Church take a deep interest in the modern world at large, an interest inspired by love.

In the modern world there is a basic fact that demands recognition: the central meaning of the Christian faith is a matter of fairly general incomprehension. This incomprehension regarding the Christian faith must, *as a matter of principle*, become *a problem for the Church herself*, under the leadership of the Church's pastoral office, not excluding the officers responsible for the safeguarding of the deposit of faith. It makes little difference whether the incomprehension is found on the part of the modern post-Christian "secularist" or the contemporary Hindu, Buddhist, or Muslim; nor has it anything to do with the question whether the secularist or the non-Christian believer are well-educated or not. It makes no difference, either, whether the incomprehension is caused by the fact that many Catholics are incapable of giving a coherent account of their faith to non-Christians (as is often the case); nor is it relevant to ask whether the incomprehension is due to prejudices on the part of the non-Christians involved (as is equally often the case). The Church simply owes the world a statement—or, more probably, a variety of statements—about the meaning of the Christian faith expressed in a way that is understandable.

Rahner's point of departure is the need for a fresh impetus to the missionary dialogue with the modern non-Christian (or post-Christian) world, in order to meet the incomprehension just described. This incomprehension among non-Christians, incidentally, is matched by widespread incomprehension on the part of Christians themselves, not excluding Catholics.

Not every Christian is equally aware of this problem,

or equally bothered by it. Pistic believers tend to be less keenly aware of it. They are protected against a sense of incomprehension by their reliance on ecclesiastical assurance, and most of the more technical doctrinal definitions do not explicitly function in their awareness. This is not to say that these "simple faithful" are irrelevant to the outside world or to the spread of the Gospel. Quite often they are exemplary, self-sacrificing Christians—still the best apology for the faith. Nevertheless, the fact that many of them are unable to give an articulate or even adequate account of the practice of their faith does remain a problem in missionary and ecumenical terms.

The situation is very different in the case of the charismatics. They often suffer quite deeply from their own lack of understanding and from their own inability to give an account of their faith-commitment without falling back on the routine phrases that they associate with their own past immaturity. They must be helped to develop an *organic* understanding of their faith, instead of being told to live with an undifferentiated collection of truths, all of them liable to be taught with equal emphasis, many of them only half understood and irrelevant to their faith-commitment, and some even downright obstacles to it.

Vatican II recognized that "Catholic belief needs to be explained more profoundly and precisely, in ways and in terminology which our separated brethren *too* can understand." And the Council went on to teach that the truths of the faith are arranged in an "order" or "hierarchy," since "they vary in their relationship to the foundation of the Christian faith."[4] It must indeed be recognized that many points of doctrine have limited theological authority; sometimes they are of almost purely historical interest. Many definitions date back to the medieval councils; they tend to counter Oriental liturgical traditionalism by means of Occidental canonical legalism. They also tend to present minor points of doctrine and discipline in a disproportionately emphatic fashion. Other definitions go back to the period between the Council of Trent and Vatican I with its tendency towards overdefinition in the interest of demarcation and polemic. It is a theological and pastoral mistake to promote an undifferentiated view of such points of doctrine and to enforce them indiscriminately as integral to the rule of faith.

In this way it turns out to be *in the interest of both the Church's openness and her identity* to develop statements of the meaning of the Christian faith that are relevant today. This requires a fundamental refusal as well as two other things.

The refusal involves the decision not to create the impression that there are doctrinal positions, whether ancient or modern, that do not stand in need of *interpretation* to be understood. Any form of doctrinal literalism or intransigence exhibited by Churches, including the Catholic Church, sets a bad example in the modern world. Churches should encourage those movements in the modern world which are promoting responsible dialogue. They should do everything possible to discontinue the false impression that the Christian faith is, among other things, the holding of a number of curious truths of much antiquity and authority, but little attractiveness or obvious relevance.

Does this mean that the Church must throw out established doctrine and trade it in for something more acceptable today? Of course not. Neither intransigence nor spineless conformity will do. Patience, of course, is a different matter. The patient can wait because they are full of *hope*. They realize that there are no short-cuts to good doctrine and that true understanding and reconciliation are not a matter of quick bargains struck at cut rates.[5] Doctrinal definitions, when properly handled and understood, function as *symbols*, symbols of hope and endurance. Hope requires that the Church remain open and hospitable to the outside world and that she let its concerns really concern her. Endurance may at times require that she keep a standoff going, and sometimes even that she provoke a conflict; but this is only legitimate on condition that she remains receptive to the world's concerns.

The two other things follow from this. Firstly, *ad extra*, the Church must foster an empathetic, questioning interest in the modern world and its concerns—an interest animated by the objectivity of love. At the intellectual level, this involves the constant practice of *cultural hermeneutic*. Rather than engage in a *forensic*, judgmental relationship to cultures, the Church must make the effort to *interpret*. Interpretation involves an effort to welcome, study, and question cultures with a view to appreciating them according to their deepest intentions. It also involves a willingness to engage in the kind of dialogue that will expose the interpreter's prejudices as well as the cultures'. Secondly, *ad intra*, it requires the constant and creative exercise of a *hermeneutic of doctrine*: the need for new formulas to convey the essence of the Christian faith to the world is also an invitation to the Church to question appreciatively the established, authoritative formulas in order to disengage their deepest intentions from the dated judgments associated with them. This will make room for new formulas that are not so much directed *against* the Tradition as designed to further it.

This in turn requires a willingness for the Church, including the Magisterium, to go beyond a purely *magisterial* reading of the Tradition and to move on to historical interpretation. In seeking to understand herself, the Church has a true *history* to understand, and this requires that she encourage within herself an interpretative dialogue with the Tradition, geared to the discovery of prejudices past as well as present.

There remains a problem, of course. New statements about the meaning of the Christian faith can never be squared with existing, authoritative ones in such a way that the new simply coincides with the old. *All* statements, whether old and magisterial or new and relevant, are "arrangements" of themes and emphases in which things are said as well as unsaid.[6] New formulas, when compared with old ones, always leave a logical gap to be bridged; and the only ways to bridge the gap are the exercise of the imagination and the active pursuit of trust. To put this differently, creedal statements old and new can only function rightly if they are allowed to function symbolically, that is to say, in an atmosphere of *communio* ultimately guaranteed by worship.

Here, it seems to me, lies a weakness in Rahner's proposal: while taking the need for intellectual integrity as seriously as everywhere else in his works, Rahner does not place enough emphasis on the original, that is to say, the *doxological* nature of viable creedal statements. Not that Rahner takes his cue only from the modern world's concerns with transcendence, humanity, and the future; in commenting on his proposals, Rahner makes a point of explaining that the Christological component is there and must not be overlooked. Still, Christology, while being indeed the central affirmation in any Creed, itself goes back to the act of worship: the sacrifice of praise and thanksgiving to the Father in the Name of Jesus acknowledged as Lord on the strength of the Holy Spirit, which is also the source of the Church's faith and identity experience. As a result, Rahner's three proposals for a Theological, an Anthropological, and a Future-Oriented Creed are too philosophical and abstract[7] to command a wide appeal as symbols. But his principle is sound. All of humanity, along with all its concerns, is to be brought into the Christian confession; and so the Church, in virtue of her very nature, has a duty to take humanity seriously, so as to enable it to hear and speak the saving word, to "each in their own language."[8]

## The Vatican Reply to ARCIC I

Let us turn to the second example, the 1982 *Reply* of the Sacred Congregation of the Doctrine of the Faith to the

*Final Report* published by ARCIC. Again, this is not the place to do complete justice to this document. To do that, a full discussion both of the ARCIC *Final Report* and the Congregation's *Reply*, as well as a meticulous comparison between the two would be necessary. Also, the present treatment does not mean to imply that the *Reply* is a document of great theological or disciplinary authority. But like Rahner's proposal for *Kurzformel*, the *Reply* affords an opportunity to discuss the issue of Catholic identity and openness in an ecumenical perspective at this time.

In order to arrive at a fair evaluation of the *Reply*, it is important to be clear from the outset about its stated limitations. The *Reply* is not meant to be a constructive document but a "doctrinal examination" prepared "at the request of the Holy Father." Hence it is a critical assessment of ARCIC, leading to certain "conclusions [. . .] set forth in [. . .] observations."[9] We should not expect, therefore, a systematic treatment, but rather a series of remarks that are likely to dwell on imperfections and unfinished business in the *Final Report*.

But even within the context of its stated limitations, we can review the *method* of the *Reply*, as well as put forward some hypotheses about the *assumptions* behind it. In these two areas, three matters are of particular interest. First, the *Reply* treats, respectively, matters of Anglican and Catholic doctrine in a comparative fashion, and this can be shown to imply a certain attitude towards ecumenical dialogue. Secondly, the *Reply* operates on the basis of a very definite, as well as very debatable conception of the "hierarchy of truths." Thirdly, the *Reply* implies a certain theory about the status of doctrinal formulas, and thus presupposes a particular conception of faith.

In its "Final Remarks,"[10] the *Reply* gives a very precise summary of its findings. It then goes on to point out that the ARCIC *Final Report* "does not yet constitute a substantial and explicit agreement on some essential elements of Catholic faith." The following points are mentioned: (a) It contains doctrines not accepted by Anglicans, such as eucharistic adoration, infallibility, and the Marian dogmas. (b) It contains doctrines which are only partly accepted, such as the primacy of the bishop of Rome. (c) It contains points formulated in a manner too ambiguous to exclude interpretations not in harmony with the Catholic faith, such as the eucharist as sacrifice, the real presence, the nature of the priesthood. (d) It contains points that are inexact and not acceptable as Catholic doctrine, such as the relationship between the structure of the Church and the primacy, and the doctrine about the "reception" of authoritative teaching. (e) Finally, there remain points of Catholic teaching the *Report* does not touch on, except perhaps indirectly, such as apostolic succession, moral teaching, and so on.

There is no doubt that the *Reply* raises several important problems. There is no doubt, either, that it operates on methods and assumptions which need to be tested.

The first point that comes to mind is that the *Reply* treats all those points in the *Final Report* which betray the presence of Anglican partners in the dialogue as ambiguities and difficulties, and it does so by pointing to items of Catholic doctrine as unambiguous and certain. This leads to a curious lopsidedness. The *Reply* regrets, on the one hand, that ARCIC has not "indicated their position in reference to the documents which have contributed significantly to the formation of the Anglican identity (*The Thirty-Nine Articles of Religion, Book of Common Prayer, Ordinal*) in those cases where the assertions of the final report seem incompatible with these documents."[11] But on the other hand, there is no parallel request for comparison with Trent. It is obviously not fair to expect from a document such as the *Reply* that it involve itself in hermeneutics. What one can expect, though, is that it recognize the need for hermeneutics. The *Reply* fails, therefore, to take seriously the task of the Catholic Church, including the Magisterium, of interpreting the affirmations of (in this case) the Anglicans in light of their own intentions. It also fails to recognize that Catholic doctrines, too, are subject to interpretation. The *Reply*, in other words, measures Anglican doctrines and Catholic doctrines with two different standards.

This is regrettable for the following reason. The *Final Report* is the *record of a dialogue*—a fact recognized and appreciated by the *Reply*.[12] Still, the way in which the *Reply evaluates* this record is not in keeping with this recognition. The *Reply* treats the ARCIC *Report*, not as the fruit of a dialogue, but as the result of a *negotiation*. There is a big difference between the two. In a dialogue partners feel responsible for each other's positions; in a negotiation each partner feels responsible only for his own. The *Reply* fosters the latter and does not encourage the former.

Secondly, the *Reply* promises that in dealing with the issues mentioned, it will deal only with "points which truly pertain to the faith," and not with secondary points, such as rites, theological opinion, church discipline, and spirituality. But it goes on explicitly to observe that in the case of those former points "it would not be possible . . . to appeal to the 'hierarchy of truths' of which Number 11 of The Decree on Ecumenism of Vatican II, *Unitatis Redintegratio*, speaks."[13] This is truly an extraordinary statement, especially if we have a look at the nature of the points discussed, summed up in the *Reply*'s "Final Remarks." Neither the context nor the record of the conciliar debates suggest that the concept of "hierarchy of truths" applies only to "secondary points." In fact, both point in the opposite direction. Johannes Feiner is only drawing the obvious conclusion from the text of the Decree as well as the conciliar record when he writes: "This hierarchy, of course, must not be arbitrarily determined. The decree itself gives the criterion: the order of doctrines in this hierarchy depends on 'their relationship to the foundation of the Christian faith.' *Thus the importance of a doctrine is not determined by the degree to which it is theologically binding, as though a defined doctrine belonged to the first rank of truths solely on the basis of the fact that it had been defined*, while a non-defined truth of revelation was *eo ipso* of a lower rank. The criterion is rather the closeness to the mystery of Christ, which of course includes the mystery of the Trinity."[14] According to the council, therefore, the "hierarchy of truths" is the fruit of the divine condescension, to which the Church responds in worship and witness. Without saying so in so many words, the Sacred Congregation's *Reply* claims that it is the product of *magisterial definition*.

This leads to the third point. The *Reply* betrays an exclusively pistic conception of faith and one that is still unduly affected by outdated cultural forms of the pistic stance—those discussed earlier in this book.[15] One of the consequences of this highly propositional and undifferentiated enforcement of the Catholic faith is most serious. The magisterial office can exercise disciplinary and even bureaucratic control over *communio* and worship, that is to say over the original experience of Catholic openness and identity, which is the baptismal birthright of every Catholic and which especially modern charismatic Catholics seek; and it can do so in the name of propositions most of which are not functional in normal, everyday ecumenical relations, and most of which are irrelevant to worship much of the time. This continues the impression given to many serious non-Catholics that the Catholic faith is largely a matter of belief in and observance of a large and unattractive and hard-to-understand body of rituals, rules, and truths authoritatively enforced. One of the things "hierarchy of truths" involves is precisely the realization that not all truths, not even all the defined ones, are communally, doxologically, and evangelically significant everywhere and all the time. Responsible Catholic participation in Christian life and work at large and, even more importantly, in Christian worship can develop only if the Catholic identity-experience is allowed to develop on grounds other than boundary-experience. One necessary precondition for this is the recapturing, by the Church's Pastoral Office, of its own central responsibility, not only for the safeguarding of tradition, but also, and especially, for worship and evangelization, in which Catholic identity and Catholic openness are not at odds with each other. The present Pope, John Paul II, is showing the Church and the world that unashamed worship and an active outreach to the world are at the heart of the Church. This, rather than magisterial enforcement of defined doctrine, will lead to sound and constructive doctrinal developments, that is to say, developments not necessarily bounded by the purview of the narrow angle set by past definitions, and hence not necessarily in strictly linear continuity with them.[16]

# Notes

## *One*

1. To mention one example, it has been convincingly argued that the Constitution on the Church and the Decree on Ecumenism, *Lumen Gentium* and *Unitatis Redintegratio*, show four distinct strains that have not been quite harmoniously interwoven: 1. the Church is the sacrament of salvation and yet a community of sinners; 2. the Church is local as well as universal; 3. the Church is both guided by the Spirit and institutional; 4. the Church is God's People moving in history. Cf. Raymond Pelly, *The Spirit, the Church and the Churches* (Unpublished doctoral dissertation, University of Geneva, 1969). Here is another example: the Council document on Revelation, *Dei Verbum*, while giving a sound and balanced account of the relationship between Scripture and Tradition, leaves unsolved some important problems regarding the authoritative interpretation of both.

2. Cf. Karl Rahner, 'Towards a Fundamental Theological Interpretation of Vatican II,' *Theological Studies*

40 (1979) 716-727; id., 'Perspektiven der Pastoral in der Zukunft', *Diakonia* 12 (1981) 221-235 (cf. *Theology Digest* 30 (1982) 59-62.)

3. J. Verhaar has pointed to the modern tendency to use words derived from the realm of technical expertise to denote the realities themselves, which the experts deal with. When a person has emotional problems, we say that he or she has "psychological" problems. When I have a hard time believing in God, I am likely to say that I have "a theological question," which, it must be admitted, sounds better. Cf. Verhaar's 'Language and Theological Method', *Continuum* 7(1969)3-29, esp. 25-26; also, 'Phenomenology as an Attitude', *Bijdragen* 28(1967)399-421.

4. For the last two paragraphs, see John Coulson's stimulating book *Religion and Imagination*, (Oxford: Oxford University Press, 1981), quotations p. 126; on 'saying and unsaying,' see pp. 63ff., and 115ff.

5. Vatican II, Dogmatic Constitution on Divine Revelation, *Dei Verbum*, 8.

6. Cf. Romans 8:26.

7. Cf. above, note 5.

8. Cf. John Henry Newman, *An Essay on the Development of Christian Doctrine*, Chapter V, Section 3; also, see Owen Chadwick, *From Bossuet to Newman, The Idea of Doctrinal Development*, (Cambridge: Cambridge University Press, 1957), p. 157; also, see F.J. van Beeck, S.J., *Christ Proclaimed—Christology as Rhetoric*, (New York: Paulist Press, 1979), p. 571; see also pp. 137-43, where the "double binding" of all theological discernments—their position between the total commitment on the one hand and the concerns of this life on the other—is discussed.

9. A fairly recent issue of *America* magazine contains three eloquent and badly needed pleas in favor of church history, by three of its most competent American practitioners: John Tracy Ellis, John W. O'Malley, S.J., and James Hennesey, S.J.; *America* 147(1982)185-93. I

use the term "succession of arrangements" rather than "development," in order not to prejudice the issue. "Development of doctrine," in fact, involves both gain of tradition and loss of tradition. Dogmatic theologians, with their tendency to construe rather than observe and interpret, tend to overlook what is obvious to the trained historian's eye, namely, that the Church's living Tradition is, in fact, a succession of "structurings." On this subject, see Paul Misner, 'A Note on the Critique of Dogmas', *Theological Studies* 34(1973)690-700.

10. For what I call a "sober-minded" passage, see the second paragraph of the Constitution on the Church, *Lumen Gentium*, nr. 14, which forms the introduction to nrs. 15ff., which treat the Catholic Church's relationships with other Christians, with all believers, and finally with all unbelievers. Rather than making exorbitant and triumphalistic claims on behalf of Catholics, the Council, in nr. 14, availed itself of the opportunity to remind Catholics that acceptance of the Catholic Church's *systemic* fullness creates no assurance of salvation, if there is no perseverance in charity.

11. 'Religious Freedom', in: Walter M. Abbott, S.J., *The Documents of Vatican II*, (New York: America Press – Chapman, 1966), p. 673.

12. W.H. van de Pol, *Het einde van het conventionele christendom*, (Roermond—Maaseik: J.J. Romen & Zonen, 1968); trans. by Theodore Zuydwijk, S.J., (Westminster, Md.: Newman Press, 1968).

13. W.H. van de Pol, *Het einde van het conventionele christendom*, pp. 32-36 (trans. pp. 22-25). The reference is to Gordon W. Allport's *The Nature of Prejudice*. If we recognize the *formal* analogy between the structure of much of the traditional Catholic faith-experience and the structure of prejudice, we will also recognize the difficulty involved in what I have called the "rearrangement of the themes and emphases of the Catholic faith-experience"; hence, we would do well to bear in mind Allport's state-

ment (van de Pol, p. 33; trans. p. 23): "To change [a prejudice], the whole pattern of life would have to be altered."

14. While legitimate questions have been raised, especially by Hans Urs von Balthasar and Bert van der Heijden, as to whether Rahner's transcendental reflection does sufficient justice to the actuality of the Christian confession, there is absolutely no doubt about Rahner's own awareness of the fact that transcendental reflection can only productively occur *within* the setting of the Christian profession of faith. Curiously, Hans Küng has attacked Rahner's conception of "anonymous Christianity": *Christ Sein*, (Munchen and Zürich: R. Piper & Co., Verlag, 1974), pp. 89-90, 118; trans.: *On Being a Christian*, (Garden City, N.Y.: Doubleday and Company, 1976) pp. 97-98, 126. It is clear that Küng misunderstands Rahner, and that his own theology presupposes the very notion he opposes in Rahner. See the debate between Heinz Robert Schlette, Küng himself, and L. Bruno Puntel in *Orientierung* 39(1975)174-176; 214-216; 40(1976)3-6.

15. Acts 4:12.

16. It may not be out of place to point out that the last opinion mentioned, while professing to put an end to the claims to superiority allegedly put forward by Christianity, involves an exercise of that very superiority: Buddhism finds itself characterized in such a way as to provide Christianity with a perfect foil of itself. The alleged parallel between Christ and the Buddha is entirely the product of a *Christian* theologian's effort to come to terms with his *own* faith. There is a great deal more merit in a patient study of Buddhism on its own terms. On this subject, see my 'Professing the Uniqueness of Christ,' *Chicago Studies* 24(1985)17-35.

17. I am especially thinking of theologians like Paul Tillich, *Christianity and the Encounter of the World Religions*, (New York: Columbia University Press, 1963), who uses notions like "ultimate concern" by way of a

common meeting-ground. John Hick (*e.g.*, 'Jesus and the World Religions', in: John Hick, ed., *The Myth of God Incarnate*, (Philadelphia: The Westminster Press, 1977), pp. 167-85, who places Jesus in the general framework of "God's dealings with us"; and Maurice Wiles, esp. *The Remaking of Christian Doctrine*, (London: SCM Press, 1974), who proposes a general scheme, strongly reminiscent of classical Deism, to interpret the Christian confession.

18. *Der antirömische Affekt. Wie lässt sich das Papsttum in der Gesamtkirche integrieren?*, (Freiburg: Herder-Verlag, 1974).

19. For a discussion of the cultural background of the tradition that produced men like Ottaviani, cf. an essay by the present author on a new edition of a book by one of Ottaviani's friends and associates, Pietro Parente's *L'Io di Cristo*: 'Reflections on a Dated Book', *The Heythrop Journal* 24(1983)51-57.

20. Cf. the poignant discussion of the problem in Jürgen Moltmann's *Der gekreuzigte Gott*, (Munchen: Chr. Kaiser Verlag, 1972), esp. pp. 12-30; English trans., *The Crucified God*, (New York: Harper & Row, 1974).

21. The book by W.H.van de Pol (above, note 12) contains a good discussion of the well-known positions of Kraemer and Soper (pp. 292-325; trans. pp. 253-81).

22. Gerard Manley Hopkins, *The Wreck of the Deutschland*, st. 27.

23. John 1:3.

24. Colossians 1:16-17.

25. On convergence as the joint operation of interiorization and complexification, see, for example, Pierre Teilhard de Chardin, *L'Activation de L'Energie*, (Paris: Editions du Seuil, 1963), (*Oeuvres*, VII), p. 375; English trans. *Activation of Energy*, (New York and London: Harcourt Brace Jovanovich, 1970), p. 356.

## *Two*

1. The inspiration behind this triple division is varied. For a brief, very incomplete indication of sources, cf. Appendix I, pp. 79-82.

2. Cf., fairly recently again, Yves Congar, 'Ministry in the Early Church and Subsequent Historical Evolution', Symposium on Ministries, Hong Kong, February 28 – March 6, 1977, *FABC*, II-2.

3. Cf. especially, Walter J. Ong, S.J., *Ramus, Method, and the Decay of Dialogue*, (Cambridge, Mass.: Harvard University Press, 1958; more recent editions available), but also his other, more recent works, among which special mention should go to *The Presence of the Word*, (New Haven and London: Yale University Press, 1967; more recently editions, as well as Italian and French translations, available).

4. Competently discussed by J.H.van den Berg, respectively in *Metabletica van de materie – Meetkundige Beschouwingen*, (Nijkerk: G.F. Callenbach, [2]1969), pp. 305ff., and *Het menselijk lichaam*, Vol. I, (Nijkerk: G.F. Callenbach, [5]1965), pp. 171ff.

5. Cf. the suggestion in Ernest L. Fortin, 'The New Rights Theory and the Natural Law', *The Review of Politics* 44(1982)590-612, esp. 601-02, which also refers to the final step set by Hobbes, in the same century, by denying that the human individual is a social being at all.

6. H. de Lubac, *The Mystery of the Supernatural*, (New York: Herder and Herder, 1967), esp. pp. 181ff.

7. Cf.: "The *combination* of oral-acoustical habits and the development of literacy as practiced and promoted by the art of printing and the habit of concentration on *texts* contributed enormously to the hardening of theological positions, in as well as among the churches, in the period between the early sixteenth century and the end of the last century or so. It is not by accident that

Walter Ong's seminal work refers to 'the Decay of Dialogue', and that he has recently argued, with ever greater variety and emphasis, that we are now moving into a new, post-literate oral-acoustical culture, which opens entirely new opportunities (and demands!) for communication. The cultural world *between* the rise of humanistic literacy on the one hand and the development of electronic communication, from Edison and Marconi on into the present, global communication by television and cybernetics on the other hand—that world was profoundly anti-dialogical and anti-ecumenical": F.J.van Beeck, S.J., 'Reflections on a Dated Book', *The Heythrop Journal* 24(1983)51-57, quotation pp. 55-56.

8. For an early exploration of the consequences of this modern *diaspora* for the Church, see Karl Rahner, "The Prospect for Christianity," in *Free Speech in the Church*, (New York: Sheed and Ward, 1959), 51-112. Not so long ago the German author Heinrich Böll reiterated his vigorous protest against the continued existence of a largely meaningless *Vorschriftenkatholizismus* ("prescription Catholicism") and against the politicizing of the Church in Germany, illustrated by the *Verquickung* ("bonding") of the Catholic Church and the Christian Democratic Union and by the collection of the *Kirchensteuer* ("Church tax") by the West German Internal Revenue Service. See '"Konflikte bewirken Literatur"—Ein Interview mit Heinrich Böll,' *Herder-Korrespondenz* 36(1982)431-36; also: '"Die mogliche Verwirkliching evangelischer Gedanken"—Interview mit Heinrich Böll: Wie er sich in der deutschen Gegenwart als Katholik versteht,' *Orientierung* 46(1982)183-87. The insinuation, expressed by Rahner and many others and repeated by Böll, that the Catholic Church authorities in Germany use the considerable wealth that comes to them from the Church tax to influence *political* developments in Third World countries while offering much-needed missionary assistance must be taken seriously. The Jesuit F. Danuwinata, writing in the Indonesian weekly *Tempo* quite

a few years ago, made an analogous observation: financial leverage enables German church authorities to determine the priorities of the Catholic Church in Indonesia. We would do well to remember that the connection between the traditional pistic type of Catholic faith-experience and the world of politics in a country like Germany has enormous repercussions, through purely political channels, in the areas of ecumenism and evangelization. Böll, Rahner, and Danuwinata may have been angry; they were not wrong.

9. *Lumen Gentium*, 7; *Ad Gentes*, 5.

10. See my *Christ Proclaimed—Christology as Rhetoric*, pp. 510-18.

11. *The Documents of Vatican II*, pp. 710-19, esp. 716ff.

12. *Lumen Gentium*, 8.

13. James Hennessey, *American Catholics*, (New York and Oxford: Oxford University Press, 1982), p. 283.

14. Hennessey mentions the fact that Catholics grew from twenty-one million to forty-two million between 1940 and 1960 (*Ibid.*).

15. *Ibid.*, pp. 307-31.

16. It will be clear that the term *charismatics*, as used in this book, does not in and of itself refer to Catholics, or Christians, connected with the charismatic renewal movement in the United States or similar movements elsewhere, whose most prominent characteristic is a free and relatively spontaneous style of community prayer. *Charismatics*, in this book, covers all Christians and Catholics who are *primarily* characterized by personal motivation and initiative in the active practice of their faith. Many of those ordinarily called "charismatics" are well within the terms of this definition. Nevertheless, I seem to have met enough members of the charismatic renewal movement, whose faith has such prominent authoritarian, fundamentalist features that the suggestion is warranted that they are really "pistics" of a rather emotional, non-institutional kind.

17. See especially I Corinthians 12-14. Also, on the whole subject of community and ministry, see Pheme Perkins, *Ministering in the Pauline Churches*, (New York: Paulist Press, 1982).

18. Title of an influential book by Henri Nouwen (Garden City, N.Y.: Doubleday, 1972).

19. See, for example, I Corinthians 8:7-13; 12:22-26.

20. At the same time I must confess that I find a fair amount of fastidiousness in what von Balthasar has to say on this score. He does not show much pastoral awareness of the problem of the widespread sense of boredom with the tradition, especially among the better educated. This is often caused by the relative unavailability of sophisticated interpretations of the Tradition. This leads me to a related suggestion. I seem to have noticed a curious byproduct of the actualism prevalent among "charismatic" Catholics, and among some authors sympathetic to their plight. I am referring to a tendency to counter the traditional, naive, undifferentiated appeals to "tradition" by citing allegedly older and more substantial traditions for polemical purposes, often in the name of "history." This often results in quite a biased reading of history, which is not preferable to the traditional absence of historical sense. It takes a refined, somewhat contemplative hermeneutic (and one which includes, among other things, a good awareness of the interpreter's own prejudices!) to read the history of the Church in such a way that it can reliably function as a criticism of the *status quo*.

21. Shades of I Corinthians again: 1:10-17! Heresy, meanwhile, is not the monopoly of the charismatics, or the "liberals," as they are usually called in this context. The traditional pistic community, too, has all kinds of heretical features, equally unintentional, or "cryptogamous," to use Rahner's phrase. We can think of popular forms of patripassionism, monophysitism, and of a magical interpretation of the sacraments in doctrinal matters; an excessive devotion to the absolutely literal text of the

liturgy and a minute execution of the rubrics in matters of worship; and of scrupulosity, serious lack of personal responsibility, and a *de facto* Pelagian attitude towards virtue in ethical matters.

22. This reluctance to make strong Christological affirmations is often connected, in my experience, with the fact that charismatics have a tendency to be reserved vis-a-vis strong affirmations about God. Cf. above, Appendix I, esp. pp. 81-2. Karl Rahner has often pointed out that the modern need for transcendental reflection necessitates a greater care in avoiding naive conceptions of God. See, for example, the strongly apophatic elements in Chapter II of his *Foundations of Christian Faith*, 'Man in the Presence of Absolute Mystery' (New York: Crossroad, 1978), pp. 44ff.).

23. On Jesus and his "cause," see my *Christ Proclaimed—Christology as Rhetoric*, pp. 148-50, 192-3. One of the abiding attractions, and limitations, of the work of Hans Küng, I find, is that he is such a perfect exponent of what I have called the charismatic experience—which also goes a long way to explain his extraordinary influence among thinking Catholics, other Christians, and open-minded agnostics. It also explains the widespread incomprehension that still surrounds his removal as a "Catholic theologian," and the suspicion with which he is still viewed by the authorities in the Church. From his early works on, his emphasis has been on actual situations, often with great benefit to the Church, as in the case of his *The Council and Reunion* (New York: Sheed and Ward, 1961), which helped set the agenda for the Council. The pluralism that is so characteristic of the charismatic attitude is evident on every page of *Structures of the Church* (New York: Crossroad, 1970) and *The Church* (New York: Sheed and Ward, 1967), though rather at the expense of focus on the Church's unity, especially in the Spirit. Personal motivation, ecumenism, evangelization, and personal responsibility are pervading themes of *On Being a Christian* (Garden City, N.Y.: Dou-

bleday & Company, 1976). Criticism of the purely pistic stance, and of too absolutist and political an approach to authority, and teaching authority in particular, have been the overtones of books like *Truthfulness: the Future of the Church* (New York: Sheed and Ward, 1968) and *Infallible* (Garden City, N.Y.: Doubleday, 1971).—I have argued that Küng's Christology in *On Being a Christian* has what might be called Pelagian overtones. The very attractive presentation of Jesus in his ministry focuses, with characteristic moral earnestness, on Jesus' significance as the past example for Christian existence and Christian commitment today; but Jesus' own prayer is hardly mentioned, the Resurrection is treated only as a fact in the past, and the Christological theme of pre-existence, while not denied, is characteristically understated (See "Küng's *Christ Sein*: A Review Article," *Andover Newton Quarterly* 16(1976)277-81).

24. For an attractive example of an attempt to view Christianity primarily as a movement, see Theo Westow, 'The Changing Shape of the Institution,' in John Dalrymple and others, *Authority in a Changing Church*, (London and Sydney: Sheed and Ward, 1968), pp. 103-37. Westow characteristically emphasizes the role of Christ as a prophet. For Böll's refusal to call himself a Christian: ". . . that is a designation meant purely to impress, and it is always connected with complacency. . . . That is why I prefer to define myself as Catholic—that is a bit dirtier, . . . a bit less complacent" (*Orientierung* 46(1982)186).

25. I Corinthians 8:12.

26. I Corinthians 12:31.

27. Above, pp. 33-4.

28. Above, pp. 32-3.

29. Above, p. 21.

30. For a fine account of this, see Thomas P. Rausch, "An Ecumenical Eucharist for a World Assembly," *America* 150(1984)25-29.

## THREE

1. Above, pp. 3-4 and note 2.

2. Cf. I Timothy 3:16.

3. Cf. I Timothy 2:4.

4. Cf. Romans 15:7-13.

5. Cf. Psalm 24:1; I Corinthians 10:26 in context.

6. It will be recalled that the Pharisees were careful to keep their distance from what they viewed as the corrupt priestly establishment associated with the Temple; their powerbase was the local community, with the synagogue as the focal point.

7. Cf. Wisdom 2, one of the main sources of the Passion narratives of the Synoptic Gospels.

8. Luke 21:19; Romans 8:18. See, for example, Romans 5:3f. and Hebrews 10:36 for the same theme.

9. Cf. Romans 10:8-9; Ephesians 1:18; II Corinthians 4:6; Philippians 2:11; I Corinthians 16:22; Revelation 22:17, 20. On boldness in speech as a fundamental feature of the Christian confession, see my *Christ Proclaimed*, pp. 109, 349-52.

10. Cf. the promise made above, pp. 9-11.

11. *Christ Proclaimed*, pp. 257-9, 260, 402-5, 457-60.

12. Above, pp. 37-8.

13. Above, pp. 32-3.

14. On this subject, see my *Grounded in Love—Sacramental Theology in an Ecumenical Perspective*, (Washington, D.C.: University Press of America, 1981), pp. 66-74.

15. See *Christ Proclaimed*, pp. 146-50, 154-6, 192-3.

16. Acts 2:32.

17. Mark 15:39; Luke 23:47.

18. Cf. Acts 1:8; Matthew 28:18-20.

19. Romans 1:4.

20. Revelation 1:5; cf. 3:14. Notice the references, in I Timothy 6:11-16, to varieties of witness in an eschatolog-

ical perspective; Jesus' martyrial acceptance of Pilate's sentence acts as the historic precedent.

21. For literal references to witness in the fourth Gospel, cf. John 8:14 and 18:37.

22. Johann Baptist Metz, *Zeit der Orden?—Zur Mystik und Politik der Nachfolge*, (Freiburg, Basel, Wien: Herder, 1977); English trans., *Followers of Christ—Religious Life and the Church*, (London and New York: Ramsey, Burns & Oates/Paulist Press, 1978); the English title does not convey the point made by the German title).

23. DS 3840-1; *AAS* 39(1947)528-9. Cf. Vatican II's Constitution on the Sacred Liturgy, *Sacrosanctum Concilium*, nr. 7.

24. I have given a fuller account of all of this in *Christ Proclaimed*, esp. pp. 117-25, 327-41, 347-54.

25. II Corinthians 4, 7. For some profound reflections on this theme, see Hans Frei, *The Identity of Jesus Christ*, (Philadelphia: Fortress Press, 1975), especially pp. 17-34, 154-65.

26. Hans Küng's plea for a sober-minded Mariology on the basis of history and Scripture, while useful to correct runaway piety and ecumenically understandable, is one of the instances of the tendency, in *On Being a Christian*, (pp. 457-62), to give a reduced account of the Christian faith, that is, an account that curtails the mystic dimension. See above, pp. 44-5 and note 23. I have elaborated the theme of what here I call "ecstatic identity" under the rubic of "responsive identity" in *Christ Proclaimed*, especially pp. 270-2, 327-9, 412-5, 423-7, 471-2.

27. *In der Fülle des Glaubens—Hans Urs von Balthasar Lesebuch*, Medard Kehl and Werner Löser, eds., (Basel, Freiburg, Wien: Herder, 1980), p. 226; English trans., *The von Balthasar Reader*, Edited by Medard Kehl and Werner Löser, translated by Robert J. Daly, S.J. and Fred Lawrence, (New York: Crossroad, 1982), p. 228.

28. Vatican II, Constitution on the Sacred Liturgy, n. 10.

29. Cf. I Corinthians 2:10-16.

30. Cf. I Corinthians 12:4-6.

31. Cf. I Thessalonians 5:19-21; I Corinthians 8:3.

32. I am not implying that this prayerlessness is the result of widespread neglect, let alone that it is intentional. I am even less advocating the introduction of emphatic ways of pushing for prayer on the part of presiders and homilists by an intentional display of affect, devotionality, or profundity. I am arguing that, *developmentally speaking*, public and private prayerfulness is becoming a crucial issue in the Catholic Church; and that, given our past, we have a lot to learn in this area. Let me give an example. Now that the Liturgy is celebrated facing the people and in the vernacular, the present need for expressiveness and the ancient theology that the priest acts *in persona Christi* are often combined to produce a striking moment at the time of the so-called "institution narrative" in the Eucharist: the priest enacts the words and gestures of Jesus at the Last Supper, often looking the congregation straight in the face and showing the bread and the wine. I think this is inappropriate. The "narrative" is in reality part of the prayer of thanksgiving addressed to the Father. The Father, therefore, should be the focus of the priest's attention *as well as the congregation's*. By turning the consecration into an expressive imitation of Christ's action, a precious opportunity for *prayer* is dropped in favor of a community interaction. Incidentally, the priest's acting *in persona Christi* also involves his praying to the Father!

33. Cf. John 14:2-3.

34. I have argued that the *act of speaking* in Christology, rather than the things said, do justice to the presence of Christ and the Father: *Christ Proclaimed*, pp. 96, 199-200, 232, and 249. I failed, in that book, to elaborate the important conclusion that deep silence can be eloquent, too. This applies especially to those among us to whom the traditional forms of prayer, whose language and imagery

are largely taken from the world of personal relationships, have become inauthentic or naive. Ralph A. Keifer has rightly pointed out that "the uncritical and unreflective use of this kind of language can be one of the most significant barriers to growth in the life of the Spirit," and has pointed to the availability of a "spirituality of mystery": 'A Spirituality of Mystery', *Spirituality Today* 33(1981)100-9; quotation 100. Michael Buckley has made a similar point. He alleges St. John of the Cross and the mystagogical theology of Karl Rahner to point a way out of atheism for those among us who are acutely aware of the "profound limitations of [our] knowledge and social situation": 'Atheism and Contemplation', *Theological Studies* 40(1979)680-99, quotation 699. I am indebted to Elizabeth A. Johnson, C.S.J., of the Catholic University of America, both for her critique of what I wrote and for these references.

35. For a brief discussion of one example of this, see above, Appendix II, pp. 83-93, especially 88-93.

36. Newspaper report on the first Peter Ainslie Lecture on Christian Unity, delivered at the Christian Temple in Baltimore, Md., on October 20, 1982. My treatment of intercommunion in *Grounded in Love* (pp. 125-48) neglects this dimension of worship and the urgency of full communion by focusing entirely on charismatic reasons for common worship by means of intercommunion. Intercommunion may often be the best we can do in practice, but that is not the best we can do.

37. Above, p. 57.

38. See *Christ Proclaimed*, pp. 328-9.

39. For this theme, see *Christ Proclaimed*, pp. 325-57.

40. Above, pp. 55ff.

41. Cf. John 6:37-40.

42. Cf. John 3:17; 8:50. Also, see *Christ Proclaimed*, pp. 473, 341-4.

43. Matthew 8:14-17, coll. Isaiah 53:4.

44. Cf. I Corinthians 12:14-26.

45. Cf. Galatians 1:10; I Corinthians 4:3. Both texts refer to Paul in the original contexts. They are here applied to the Church as a whole. For the theme of freedom vis-a-vis the powers that be, see the Pauline theme of "judging all things" (I Corinthians 2:15) and "judging angels" (*Ibid.* 6:3), and, of course, Galatians, *passim*.

46. Cf. above, pp. 32-3.

47. On patience and hospitality and their connection with hope, see *Christ Proclaimed*, pp. 464-518, and somewhat more remotely, pp. 519-75.

48. See above, pp. 19-20, 24-7, on boundaries, negotiation, and political associations, and on the need for an openness less dependent on negotiation.

49. On the normativity of the pistic experience and the exaggerated definitions produced by the period between Trent and the late nineteenth century, see above, pp. 28-9.

50. Two concrete examples of what I mean are treated in Appendix II, above, pp. 83-5.

## *Appendix One*

1. For Clement's picture of the true gnostic, see 'On Spiritual Perfection'—Book VII of the *Stromateis*—in *Alexandrian Christianity*, John E.L. Oulton and Henry Chadwick, eds., The Library of Christian Classics, Vol. II, (Philadelphia: The Westminster Press), pp. 93-165. A reading of nr. 57 of Book VII, pp. 128-9, will show how Clement thinks of the Christian life in terms of a progression from faith through knowledge to love, and how it is love that characterizes the true gnostic.

2. Quoted by Beryl Smalley, *The Study of the Bible in the Middle Ages*, (Notre Dame, Ind.: University of Notre Dame Press, 1964, [3]1978), p. 245.

3. For a rendition of this tradition based on texts by St. Thomas Aquinas and St. Aelred of Rievaulx, see

Aelred Squire, *Asking the Fathers*, (Wilton, Conn. and New York: Morehouse-Barlow Co., / Paulist Press, [2]1976), pp. 205-7. The description culminates in St. John of the Cross's account of the three nights.

4. 'Sacramenten en Kerk,' *Bijdragen* 18(1956)391-418; summary in French: 'Sacraments et Eglise—Droit-Culte-Pneuma,' *ibid.* 418.

5. Cf. *Christ Proclaimed—Christology as Rhetoric*, (New York: Paulist Press, 1979), *passim*.

6. Bern und München, Francke Verlag, 1973.

## *Appendix Two*

1. Above, pp. 76-7.

2. See, for instance, the Epilogue, entitled "Brief Creedal Statements," in *Foundations of Christian Faith—An Introduction to the Idea of Christianity*, (New York: Crossroad, 1978), pp. 448-60.

3. For the text of the *Reply* to the ARCIC *Final Report* by the Sacred Congregation for the Doctrine of the Faith: see, for instance, *Ecumenical Trends* 11(1982)165-71. The *Final Report* of ARCIC, released on March 31, 1982, has been published in the United States by Forward Movement Publications in Cincinnati, Ohio, and by the Office of Publishing Services of the United States Catholic Conference in Washington, D.C.

4. See the Decree on Ecumenism, *Unitatis Redintegratio*, nr. 11. I have italicized "too," to show that the Council had both Catholics and other Christians in mind. Restatement of the faith serves both Catholics and non-Catholic Christians, and, as I am arguing, the non-Christian world as well.

5. For patience and endurance as a remedy against liberalism, see *Christ Proclaimed*, pp. 516-8.

6. See above, pp. 5-6. I have argued *(Christ Proclaimed*, pp. 508-10, 520-3, 566-75,) that past doctrine must not be in a position to prevent the integration of new themes

into the Christian faith, that development of doctrine is the record of the Church's past hospitality to culture, and that there are deeper norms for good doctrinal development than immediately obvious congruence with the Tradition.

7. Rahner is perfectly aware of this; see *Foundations of Christian Faith*, p. 454. P. Schoonenberg has an alternative Creedal Formula at the end of his *The Christ* (New York: Herder and Herder, 1971), pp. 187-88; it adheres very closely to the literary form of the Apostles' Creed, and hence, it betrays the Creed's origin in worship.

8. Acts 2:11.

9. See the explanation in the introductory paragraph of the *Reply*.

10. *Reply*, under D, 1.

11. *Ibid.*, A, 2, iii.

12. Cf. *Ibid.*, A, 1; D, 2, a.

13. *Ibid.*, A, 2, ii.

14. "Commentary on the Decree [on Ecumenism]" in *Commentary on the Decrees of Vatican II*, edited by Herbert Vorgrimler, Vol. II, (New York: Herder and Herder, 1968), pp. 57-158, quotation p. 119 (italics mine). The entire section on Nr. 11 of the Decree (pp. 114-21) leaves one in no doubt on the issue as to what Vatican II meant by "hierarchy of truths"; the conciliar interventions of Bishops De Smedt and Pangrazio, quoted by Feiner, are of particular clarity and incisiveness.

15. See above, pp. 24-34.

16. See *Christ Proclaimed*, pp. 513-5. After the first draft of this book was finished, an important article by Heinrich Fries came to my attention, 'Das Petrusamt im anglikanisch-katholischen Dialog,' *Stimmen der Zeit* 107(1982)723-38 (see *The Tablet* of December 13, 1982, for a note). Apart from expressing substantial disagreements with the *Reply* very similar to the ones detailed in the present book, Fries' article suggests, by means of frequent references to fairly recent publications by Cardinal Joseph

Ratzinger, that the *Reply* should not unconditionally be assumed to have been the Cardinal's work. More recent Roman reactions to a book co-authored by Rahner and Fries, however, seem to point in a different direction.